Lord, I Want to
Be Whole

Lord, I Want to Be Whole

*The Power of Prayer and Scripture
in Emotional Healing*

Stormie Omartian

THOMAS NELSON PUBLISHERS
Nashville

Published in Nashville, Tennessee, by Thomas Nelson, Inc.

Unless otherwise noted, Scripture quotations are from THE NEW KING JAMES VERSION. Copyright © 1979, 1980, 1982, 1990 Thomas Nelson, Inc.

Scripture quotations noted NIV are from the HOLY BIBLE: NEW INTERNA-TIONAL VERSION®. Copyright © 1973, 1978, 1984 by International Bible Society. Used by permission of Zondervan Publishing House. All rights reserved.

Some of this book's content was previously published as *Finding Peace for Your Heart*.

Library of Congress Cataloging-in-Publication Data

Omartian, Stormie

    Lord, I want to be whole : the power of prayer and scripture in emotional healing / Stormie Omartain.

      p. cm.

    ISBN 0-7852-6703-4

    1. Mental health—Religious aspects—Christianity. 2. Christian women—Religious life. I. Title.

BT732.4 .O43 2001

248.8'6—dc21

00-045227

CIP

Printed in the United States of America

1 2 3 4 5 6 PHX 05 04 03 02 01 00

To all who suffer with any kind of emotional pain or the
frustration of unfulfillment.

Through this book may God comfort your heart,
give you renewed hope,
grow you into all you can be,
and help you to find wholeness and total restoration.

CONTENTS

ACKNOWLEDGMENTS

To my husband, Michael, for his
faithfulness to God and to me.

To my sons, Christopher and John David,
and my daughter, Amanda, for giving me joy.

To Pastor Jack Hayford, for teaching me God's Word in
such power that it has changed my life forever.

To my editor extraordinaire, Janet Thoma,
for being both brilliant and compassionate.

To my aunt, Jean Davis, for a lifetime of
understanding and encouragement.

To my prayer partners, Susan Martinez, Ron Thompson,
and Katie Stewart, for all your love and support.

Steps to Emotional Health

*Y*ou're worthless, and you'll never amount to anything," my mother said as she pushed me into the little closet underneath the stairway and slammed the door. "Now stay in there until I can stand to see your face!" The sound of her footsteps faded as she walked down the small hallway back to the kitchen.

I wasn't really sure what I had done to warrant being locked in the closet again, but I knew it must be bad. I knew *I* must be bad, and I believed that all the negative things she had ever said about me were surely accurate. After all, she was my mother.

The closet was a small, rectangular storage area underneath the stairs where the dirty laundry was kept in an old wicker basket. I sat on top of the pile of clothes and pulled my feet in tight to eliminate the possibility of being touched by the mice that periodically streaked across the floor. I felt lonely, unloved, and painfully afraid as I waited in that dark hole for the seemingly endless amount of time it took for her to remember I was there or for my father to return, at which time she would make sure I was let out. Either event would mean my release from the closet and from the devastating feeling of being buried alive and forgotten.

As you can probably tell from just this one incident, I was raised by a mentally ill mother, and, among other atrocities, I spent much of my early childhood locked in a closet. Although certain people were aware of her bizarre behavior from time to time, her mental illness wasn't clearly identified until I was in my late teens. During all my growing-up years, my mother's extremely erratic behavior left me with feelings of futility, hopelessness, helplessness, and deep emotional pain. So much so that by the time I was a young woman I was still locked in a closet—only the boundaries were emotional rather than physical. I was walled in by a deep, ever-present pain in my soul, which expressed itself through certain acts of self-destruction and a paralyzing fear that controlled my every breath.

I threw myself into anything I thought would help me get free of all that—Eastern religions, occult practices, psychotherapy, unhealthy relationships, and a short, ill-fated marriage. When it became obvious that each of these things fell far short of meeting my desperate needs, I sank deeper into depression. I turned to drugs and alcohol with dangerous frequency in hopes of momentarily transcending this chronic emotional torture. Through it all I was determined to find a way out of the pain if it killed me. A few times it nearly did. By the time I was twenty-eight, suicide was the only solution I could see.

I revealed the details of this life of devastation and journey to emotional restoration in my autobiography, *Stormie.* After I wrote this book, I was deluged with letters from people telling me of their similar emotionally traumatic circumstances.

Many women said, "I just want to be whole. You've shown me for the first time that it is possible to be free of emotional pain. But now that I know there is hope for my life, what steps can I take to experience the same healing you've found?" I was asked that question time and again, and I tried to answer each individual as best I could. But there wasn't enough time or space to address the questions adequately in a letter. Telephone calls and personal contact also proved far too time consuming. I knew I needed to put all the information I had on the subject in a book, which could be read and referred to as the desire presented itself. This is that book.

What Is Emotional Health?

Many people look upon their emotional state with resignation: "This is just the way I am" or "I guess I'll have to live with it, because this is as good as it gets." Others believe that while there may be a way to make essential changes, one has to be either very spiritual or wealthy enough to afford the best professional help. "Emotional health," one girl told me, "is a remote ideal that many people want but very few people achieve."

My definition of emotional health is having total peace about who you are, what you're doing, and where you're going, both individually and in relationship to those around you. In other words, it's feeling totally at peace about the past, present, and future of your life. It's knowing that you're in line with God's ultimate purpose for you and being fulfilled in that. When you have that kind of peace and you no longer live in emotional agony, then you are a success.

In contrast to what many people think, emotional health is just as practical and attainable as physical health. If you don't feed your body the right food, you will become ill and die. Spiritually, emotionally, and mentally, you have to be fed and cared for properly, or that part of you gets sick and dies a slow death. Proper exercise for the mind and emotions is just as beneficial as exercise for the body, but most people tend not to think of it that way.

In my first book, *Greater Health God's Way*, I wrote about what I learned regarding proper care of the physical body. I'm not a nutritionist, doctor, physical therapist, or health expert. I'm simply someone who was very sick, weak, and miserable for the first twenty-eight years of her life and who then discovered a way of living that worked. In *Greater Health God's Way*, I laid down seven steps to health and instructed readers to take one step at a time in each of the seven areas, reminding them that "Everything you do counts. It will either count for life or it will count for death." I have found that the same is true for emotional health. Just as I have a physical health plan, I have a plan for emotional health. I am not a psychiatrist, psychologist, professional counselor, or pastor. I am simply a person who lived with depression, fear, suicidal thoughts, hopelessness, and intense emotional pain every day. I no longer live with any of those things. This book suggests seven steps to emotional health.

Seven Steps to Emotional Health

Your mind and emotions, like your physical body, need to be freed from stress, fed properly, exercised, cleansed, nurtured, retrained, exposed to freshness and light, and given rest. Here are seven steps that will help you to do all these things:

Step One: Release the Past
Confess to God the times you have failed, and release the times others have failed you by moving in full forgiveness.

Step Two: Live in Obedience

Understand that God's rules are for your benefit, and try to the best of your knowledge to live His way, knowing that every step of obedience brings you closer to total wholeness.

Step Three: Find Deliverance

Recognize who your enemy is, and separate yourself from anything that separates you from God or keeps you from becoming all He made you to be.

Step Four: Seek Total Restoration

Refuse to accept less than all God has for you, and remember that finding wholeness is an ongoing process.

Step Five: Receive God's Gifts

Acknowledge the gifts God has given to you, and take the steps necessary to receive them.

Step Six: Reject the Pitfalls

Avoid or get free of the negative traps and deceptions that rob you of life.

Step Seven: Stand Strong

Believe that as long as you stand with God and don't give up, you win.

These seven steps are really natural laws that work for our benefit when we live in harmony with them. Living the right way generates life, no matter who we are or what our circumstances. Likewise, doing the wrong thing leads to death.

You don't learn the seven steps in a week; they are a way of life. Understanding them with your mind will influence the state of your heart, which will affect your emotions and ultimately your entire life. Please know that I didn't master these steps overnight—and you won't either. In fact, I still work on them the same way I work toward physical health. But I have tested this plan repeatedly over the past thirty years, and I have seen these steps operate successfully in my life and the lives of countless others. The plan will be as reliable and consistent as you are in following it. I will walk through the seven steps with you just as I did on my journey toward emotional health. Together we will take it a step at a time.

What You Should Expect

In the following chapters you will find three types of information. One type is *familiar* and seems obvious, but don't be deceived by that. The familiar and obvious are often overlooked for just that reason. You may be tempted to say, "I already know I'm supposed to forgive." But the question is, are you thorough and persistent in doing it? Do you realize that it is sometimes a *process*? Did you know that you can never have emotional wholeness as long as there is unforgiveness in *any* part of your life?

The second type of information is *unfamiliar.* You've never heard it before. Or if you *have* heard it, you didn't understand its significance for your own life or that it is a requirement for emotional restoration. Did you realize that you are hindering your emotional healing by having in your house things that carry negative mental or emotional attachments? Letters from an old boyfriend, for example, can subtly perpetrate feelings of failure, sadness, hurt, or depression. It may be that such information is keeping you from the peace and fulfillment you desire.

The third type of information is *uncomfortable*. It's the kind you don't want to hear. You may react to it by saying, "I don't want to know about this because I don't want to do it." Remember how hard it was to learn you couldn't have all the candy bars and ice cream you wanted and how you paid for it when you went ahead and ate them anyway? Believe me, I understand how hard certain things are to hear and how difficult their accomplishment seems to be. But I would be less than a help to you if I were not to give you the *whole* truth. If I left out some of the pieces, you would have an incomplete plan for emotional restoration, and you'd live in frustration trying to find the missing piece. So I'm going to tell it to you as straight as I know how, and it's up to you to choose to do it or not. *Remember, you do the choosing. God working in you, as you allow Him entrance, makes it happen in your life.*

It takes a while to put these seven steps into practice and make them a way of life. How long it takes depends on how committed you are to doing what's necessary to see it happen. It also depends on how deep your emotional damage is. The degree of pain we live with today is determined by the degree of hurt we've had in our past and how early in life it occurred. The earlier it happened, the more foundational it is, and the more difficult it is to rectify. However, you have not been put on this earth just to exist or survive. You are here to have a life of purpose and meaning. No matter how much has happened to you, how young you were when it happened, or how old you are now, you can still be made whole. Don't settle for anything less.

The healing and restoration I found is there for you too. Whether your hurt is from scars from as far back as early childhood abuse or from this week's untimely severing of a precious relationship, you *can* be a whole person. You don't have to live in fear; you don't have to be depressed; you don't have to feel inadequate, stupid, untalented, or rejected. You don't have to put up with chronic emotional pain. It's possible to be free of all that.

But once you *are* healed, don't be misled into thinking you will never have a problem again. It just isn't so. Problems are a part of life in this world. You can be devastated by them, or you can meet them head-on and make them work for you rather than against you. That's why even after you are free of damaged emotions, you still must be on a maintenance program.

My journey from brokenness to wholeness didn't happen overnight. In fact, it took fourteen years for me to become pain-free and able to help others with the same problems. I believe it could have happened much faster if I had figured out what I was supposed to be doing a lot sooner. I hope this book will speed up the process for you.

Throughout our journey together I will suggest prayers for you to say that helped me in my healing process. I will also include Scriptures on the "What the Bible Says About" pages that offered me hope and encouragement. Prayer and Scripture have been important keys to my healing.

As you move into the Seven Steps to Emotional Health, don't wait until you have mastered one step before you move on to the next. Rather, begin to take a step at a time in each of the seven areas. When you do, you'll see that, though there are choices for you to make and simple steps for you to take, you don't have to be the one to make it all happen.

And remember that emotional wholeness is a process that involves changing habits of thinking, feeling, or acting. The seven steps are not a quick fix but are a way to permanently transform your inner being; that takes time.

What the Bible Says About Emotional Health

The preparations of the heart
belong to man.
—Proverbs 16:1

"For I will restore health to you
And heal you of your wounds,"
says the LORD.
—Jeremiah 30:17

I am feeble and severely broken;
I groan because of the
turmoil of my heart.
—Psalm 38:8

He restores my soul.
—Psalm 23:3

Step One: Release The Past

I'd like to make an appointment with the doctor," I said to his stern assistant over the phone. It was my first attempt to seek professional help since I'd left college a few years before.

"What is the nature of the problem?" she asked matter-of-factly.

"Well, I'd rather talk about it with the doctor," I said meekly, not sure how to verbalize the complexities of my situation.

"I preview all cases before the doctor sees them," she said tersely. "I can't make an appointment for you unless I know the nature of your problem."

"I see. Okay. Well, I was raised by an abusive mother. Her hatred expressed toward me has caused me to be extremely depressed and unable to function well and . . ."

"It is our policy that we do not accept the story of child abuse," she interrupted in her businesslike voice. "We believe it is all in the mind of the child, and it is our job to help you adjust your thinking to what is reality."

I was stunned and speechless as if I had been slapped in the face. After finally mustering up enough courage to call this highly recommended psychologist, I was being told that everything that had happened to me was all in my mind.

"You're saying that I imagined these things?" I said carefully so as not to reveal my inner anger.

"Let's just say you *think* you've been abused. We can help you straighten out your thinking."

"Oh, I see. Thank you. That's all I need to know," I said, and hung up before she had a chance to say any more. Devastated, I sat for a few moments and then felt the all-too-familiar constriction in my throat. I had always feared that if I let go and cried to the depth of my feelings, I would die from it. So I held it all back in my throat.

I fell over onto my bed and doubled up with the pain. I wished I'd never heard of this doctor. Several of my friends had recommended him after I made slight reference to my relationship with my mother. Even though I'd been out of the house for years and traveled all over the world, I couldn't get far enough away from her to eliminate her influence from my life. It looked as if the past would follow me forever unless I found some way to disconnect myself from it.

Now I felt even more hopeless. There was nowhere to turn. I mistakenly believed that this was the policy of all counselors, and so I resolved never to seek counseling again. I had been to numerous psychiatrists and psychologists before, but I had not told them about my mother's abusive behavior. It was humiliating to talk about it, and I was afraid they might think I was the crazy one. I was left feeling that suicide was my only option.

It was at that point that a friend took me to meet with her pastor, Pastor Jack Hayford at The Church on the Way. He told me about the wholeness and peace I could find by receiving Jesus into my life. I wanted that more than anything, so I received Him as my Savior. I didn't know whether that would work, but I was willing to try anything. And receiving Jesus was the only thing I hadn't tried at this point. I had sought solace in the occult, drugs, alcohol, Eastern religions, and unhealthy relationships. Each of these gave temporary relief but eventually made matters worse. This "Jesus thing" sounded like a long shot, but with suicide as the only alternative I could see, I had nothing to lose. And if Pastor Jack was right, I had everything to gain. I was quite amazed that, after I received Jesus in Pastor Jack's office, I felt hope for the first time I could remember. As it turned out, this was the beginning point of my healing. I started attending church, reading the Bible, and praying every day. I began to see light at the end of the dark tunnel of my life. I even found the man I would eventually marry sitting behind me in church one Sunday morning.

After Michael and I were married and I felt safe enough to tell him about my early childhood, he insisted that I see a counselor at The Church on the Way. He assured me that I could trust her. I had seen other counselors there for my never-ending depression, and although they never reached the core of my problem, each one was instrumental in beginning to crack the wall and open me up to the massive deliverance I would experience with this new counselor. Mary Anne would become God's instrument to help me release my past.

The Foundation of Confession

"I have these depressions that happen frequently, like emotional blackouts that last as long as two weeks at a time," I told Mary Anne at my first appointment. Her beautiful, compassionate face invited my complete trust. "I can hardly function, and my thoughts often turn to suicide as the only way out. I can't even get out of bed, except for the basic necessities of life. What's the matter with me? . . . I have the Lord, a good husband, a home, and no financial worries for the first time in my life. I read God's Word and I pray. Why is this still happening?"

"Tell me about your childhood, Stormie," she said softly. "What was it like?"

Because I felt safe with her, I told more about my past than I had ever revealed to anyone. She listened for nearly half an hour, speaking only to ask a question or two. When I was finished she said very directly, "You have bondage, Stormie, and you need deliverance."

I have what? I need what? I thought.

Mary Anne must have read my expression, because she quickly added, "It's nothing to be afraid of. Bondage is the oppression that comes upon us when we don't live the way we're supposed to. Deliverance breaks that oppression."

Then she instructed me, "I want you to go home and write down every sin God brings to your mind. Ask God to help you remember each incident, and as you write it down say, 'God, I confess this before You and ask Your forgiveness.'"

"I thought I was forgiven of all my sins when I received Jesus," I said politely, not wanting to seem uncooperative.

"That's right, you have been. But often we live right in the middle of things from which God has liberated us. Jesus' death on the cross means He took all that we had coming to us, which is death, and in return He gave us all that He had coming to Him, which is eternal life. Receiving Him means being freed from this death grip. However, the bondage that accompanies each sin must have a point of severance through confession. Whatever you confess before God will release you from the bondage that accompanies it. So go home, confess everything, and then come back in a week and we'll pray about all of it."

How well she must have me sized up, I thought as I left her office, pondering all she instructed me to do. *She knows it's going to take a week of writing to get all my sins down on paper!* Mary Anne had assured me that the paper would not be used against me at a later date, so I agreed to it.

I'd had enough good teaching at The Church on the Way to know the word *sin* is an old archery term, meaning "to miss the bull's-eye." Anything other than dead center is sin. So sin in our lives doesn't just mean robbing a liquor store, murdering someone, or playing cards on Sunday. It's much more than that. In fact, anything off the center of God's best and perfect will for our lives is sin. That takes in a lot of territory!

"I also want you to fast for three days prior to coming back," Mary Anne continued.

She wants me to fast? I gasped to myself. I'd heard about fasting from Pastor Jack, and the whole church was fasting every Wednesday, but I wasn't ready for that. Besides, I was afraid of being hungry, since I'd gone to bed too often that way as a child.

"There's a certain kind of release that will not happen without fasting and prayer, Stormie," Mary Anne explained. "It's an act of denying yourself and placing God at the center of your life, which breaks any hold that Satan has on you and destroys the bondage resulting from sin."

I need that, I thought. *It might not happen unless I fast, so I've got to do it.* I agreed and left to go home.

In those days of dark depression, I was so drained of energy that I had to take a nap before I could even begin to think about doing anything as mentally exhausting as making a list of my failures and sins. But once I woke up from my nap, I was able to quickly come up with a sizable number of obvious failures, even before I got around to asking the Lord to show me any *hidden* sins.

Just when I thought that surely I had nothing more to confess, I read in the Bible, "If we say that we have no sin, we deceive ourselves, and the truth is not in us. If we confess our sins, He is faithful and just to forgive us our sins and to cleanse us from all unrighteousness" (1 John 1:8–9). In spite of the fact that I had confessed so much already, I knew I was kidding myself to think there wasn't more. In fact, God must have known I couldn't possibly do it all in one week, so on the morning I was supposed to return to Mary Anne's office, she called to say she was ill and asked if we could reschedule for the following week.

I was terribly disappointed, especially since I'd been fasting for three days, but also because my depression had become unbearable. But with no other recourse, I continued my listing and confessing. The pile of papers grew as incidents I hadn't thought of in years flooded my mind!

I soon realized that unconfessed sin is like carrying around heavy bags of garbage. The heavier they get, the weaker we become—until we are crippled under the weight of it all. I was to know the full sense of that truth when I returned to the counseling office.

"Do you have your list?" Mary Anne asked as she smiled and held out her hand.

"Yes," I replied sheepishly. I showed her my mound of papers, embarrassed by the prospect of having her learn the full extent of the awful truth.

"Good," she said and summoned another counselor to

the room. I immediately imagined that she was summoning reinforcements in case she gave out during the hours it would take to pray about it all. Much to my surprise and relief, she and the other counselor simply put one hand on me and one hand on the papers. They didn't show the slightest interest in reading them. "Did you confess each sin as it came to mind?" Mary Anne questioned.

"Yes, I did," I nodded.

"Then lift them up to the Lord, confess it all as sin, and ask for God's forgiveness. We are going to pray for God to release you from the destruction that all this has brought upon your life."

I did what they instructed, and as they prayed I felt a distinct physical release from my head, neck, and shoulders. The headache I'd had for days disappeared, new strength came into my body, and I felt lighter and cleaner than I ever remembered feeling in my life.

The Weight of Unconfessed Sin

When sin is left unconfessed, a wall goes up between you and God. Even though the sin may have stopped, it will still weigh you down, dragging you back toward the past you are trying to leave behind. I know, because I used to carry around a bag of failures on my back that was so heavy I could barely move. I didn't realize how spiritually stooped over I had become. When I confessed my sins that day, I actually felt the weight being lifted.

Often we fail to see ourselves as responsible for certain actions. For example, while it's not your fault that someone abused you, your *reaction* to it now is your responsibility. You may feel justified in your anger or bitterness, but you still must confess it because it misses the mark of what God has for you. If you don't, its weight will eventually crush you. When you do confess, it leads to life.

For confession to work, repentance must go along with it. *Repentance* literally means "a change of mind." It means to turn your back, walk away, and decide not to do it again. It means getting your thinking aligned correctly with God. It's possible to confess without really ever conceding any fault at all. In fact, we can become simply good at apologizing with no intent of being any other way. Confession and repentance mean saying, "This is my fault. I'm sorry about it, and I'm not going to do it anymore."

I had openly confessed my sins to God as I wrote them down before that second counseling session. But once the counselors prayed for me, I had a deep sense of being forgiven. Then Mary Anne challenged me to forgive my mother.

The Foundation of Ongoing Forgiveness

Forgive someone who treated me with hatred and abuse? Someone who has ruined my life by making me into an emotional cripple? How can I? I thought, overwhelmed at the prospect of so great a task. I had already confessed my sins, and now Mary Anne was asking me to forgive my mother—all in the same counseling session. *Shouldn't this take months, even years, of therapy?*

"You don't have to *feel* forgiveness in order to say you forgive someone," Mary Anne explained. "Forgiveness is something you do out of obedience to the Lord because He has forgiven *you*. You have to be willing to say, 'God, I confess hatred for my mother, and I ask your forgiveness. I forgive her for everything she did to me. I forgive her for not loving me, and I release her into Your hands.'"

As difficult as it was, I did as she said. I wanted to forgive my mother even though I felt nothing close to that at the time. "God, I forgive my mother," I said at the end of the prayer. I knew that the power of God must be working in my life for me even to be able to say those words. And I felt His love at that moment more than I ever had before.

The next morning after this counseling and deliverance time with Mary Anne, I awoke with no depression or suicidal thoughts. It felt odd because as far back as I could remember I'd always had them. Even more surprising was that the next morning and the next and the next, there was still no depression. In fact, I never suffered from that kind of depression again. At times I have felt depressed temporarily, but since that day, depression has never controlled or paralyzed me.

I soon learned, however, that unforgiveness as deeply rooted as mine toward my mother must be unraveled, one layer at a time. This was especially true for me, since my mother's verbal abuse only continued to increase in intensity toward me. After every verbal assault, I would feel that same anger, hatred, and unforgiveness toward her. I had to learn to take charge of my will and deliberately say, "Lord, my desire is to forgive my mother. Help me to forgive her completely."

Over the next couple of years, I did this more often than I can begin to count. One day as I was again asking God to give me a forgiving heart, I felt led to pray, "Lord, help me to have a heart like *Yours* for my mother."

Almost immediately I had a vision of her as I had never seen before. She was a beautiful, fun-loving, gifted woman who bore no resemblance to the person I knew. My understanding told me I was seeing her the way God had made her to be and not the way she had become. What an amazing revelation! I couldn't have conjured it up myself. Nothing had ever surpassed my hatred for my mother, except perhaps the depth of my own emptiness. Yet now I felt compassion and sympathy for her.

I put together the pieces of her past—the tragic and sudden death of her mother when she was eleven; the suicide of her beloved uncle and foster father a few years later; her feelings of abandonment, guilt, bitterness, and unforgiveness, which contributed to her emotional and mental illness. I could see how her life, like mine, had been twisted and deformed by circumstances beyond her control. Suddenly I no longer hated her for it. I felt sorry for her instead.

Being in touch with the heart of God for my mother brought such forgiveness in me that when she died a few years later, I had absolutely no bad feelings toward her. Although her mental illness and irrational behavior had continued to worsen, which kept us from any kind of reconciled relationship, I harbored no bitterness, and I have none to this day. In fact, the more I forgave her, the more the Lord brought to mind good memories. I was amazed that there were any at all.

Stairway to Wholeness

Forgiveness leads to life. Unforgiveness is a slow death. It doesn't mean you aren't saved, and it doesn't mean you won't go to heaven. But it does mean you can't have all that God has for you and you will not be free of emotional pain.

The first step to forgiving is to *receive God's forgiveness* and let its reality penetrate the deepest part of our being.

When we realize how much we have been forgiven, it's easier to understand that we have no right to pass judgment on one another. Once we are forgiven and released from everything we've ever done wrong, how can we refuse to obey God when He asks us to forgive others? Easy! We focus our thoughts on the person who has wronged us rather than on the God who makes all things right.

Forgiveness is a two-way street. God forgives you, and you forgive others. God forgives you quickly and completely upon your confession of wrongdoing. You are to forgive others quickly and completely, whether they admit failure or not. Most of the time people don't feel they've done anything wrong anyway, and if they do, they certainly don't want to admit it to you.

Forgiveness is a choice that *we* make. We base our decision not on what we *feel* like doing but on what we *know* *is right.* I did not *feel* like forgiving my mother. Instead I *chose* to forgive her because God's Word says, "Forgive, and you will be forgiven" (Luke 6:37). That verse also says that we shouldn't judge if we don't want to be judged ourselves.

It was hard for me to understand that God loved my mother as much as He loves me. He loves *all* people as much as He loves me. He loves the murderer, the rapist, the prostitute, and the thief. And He hates their murdering, raping, whoring, and stealing as much as He hates my pride, gossiping, and unforgiveness. We may sit and compare our sins to other people's and say, "Mine aren't so bad," but God says they all stink so we shouldn't worry about whose smell the worst. The most important thing to remember about forgiveness is that *forgiveness doesn't make the other person right; it makes you free.*

Forgiving the Abuser

You may feel that the abusive person in your life is an obstacle to your freedom and healing, but that's not true. Your unforgiveness is. You can never be completely released from, or reconciled to, a person you haven't forgiven. You have to be willing to say, "Lord, I choose to forgive this person. Help me to forgive her (him) completely." When you do that, the cleansing process has begun. That's because *the law of the Lord is to let go, not get even.*

If you forgive one day and then the next day you find you are still angry, hurt, and intensely bitter toward that same person, don't be discouraged. Continue to take it to the Lord again and again. There are times we can forgive quickly, but usually forgiving a person who has caused deep wounds is an ongoing, step-by-step process. This is especially true if there has been no reconciliation. You will know the work is complete when you can honestly say you want God's best for that person. If you are living in a continually abusive relationship, find a way to separate yourself from the abuser. The antidote for poisoning doesn't work as well if you are continuing to take the posion.

A young girl named Donna came to me for help. "My father raped me many times," she cried as she told me about her past. "Because of him I'm an emotional cripple. I can never forgive him."

I gave Donna some time to recover from the pent-up emotion that was released when she told me about this. Then I said, "Donna, you have every right to feel the way you do. What was done to you was horrible. You've been so beaten down and destroyed by your dad that you can't even bring yourself to say the word *forgive* in the same sentence with his name. But tell God how you feel. He understands.

Say: 'God, I don't have any love for my dad, and I feel hurt when I even think of him. I don't want to forgive him or pray for him. In fact, part of me wants him to pay for what he has done. But because You have asked me to, I pray that You will bless him and lead him into full knowledge of You. Let him become the person You created him to be. I refuse to hold him to myself with unforgiveness. I release him to You and choose to forgive him this day. O Lord, work complete forgiveness in my heart.'"

Forgiving our parents is one of the most important things we can do, since Scripture says: "Honor your father and your mother, that your days may be long upon the land which the LORD your God is giving you" (Ex. 20:12). Forgiving them is part of that honoring and will affect the length and quality of our lives.

Pastor Jack Hayford said something that affected me profoundly with regard to forgiving my own mother. He said, "You grow up to hate yourself when you hate your parents, because what you see of them in yourself you will despise." If you despise something in yourself, check to see if it's because it reminds you of one of your parents. If so, there may be an area of unforgiveness there.

I've found that the best way to turn anger, bitterness, hatred, and resentment for someone into love is to pray for that person. God softens your heart when you do. It also helps you to remember that we will *all* stand before the same judgment seat and no one gets away with sin. We *all* eventually pay for it. If you feel that a certain abusive person is not paying enough, remember that God will not punish you or me as much as we deserve either.

When you have been badly wounded, it's important not only to forgive the person who hurt you but also to forgive each event as it comes to mind. In other words, be specific about addressing each one of your wounded places. I had to forgive every incident with my mother as I remembered it or as it was happening. Every time I forgave, it helped me to let go of more of the past and move on with my life.

You may feel that the abuse in your past has kept you from becoming all you were supposed to be. But it's really the unforgiveness for the abuse that keeps you from becoming all that God made you to be. Unforgiveness can lead to your being an abusing parent, no matter how good your intentions are. Or you may have a hard time dealing with your own anger if you don't forgive your father's angry outbursts toward you. Giving your life to God and living His way will insure that you become all you were created to be, no matter what has happened to you. That's because of God's miraculous ability to meet you right where you are and transform your life.

If *you* have done things to others that were hurtful and need to be forgiven, first ask for the Lord's forgiveness and then ask for forgiveness from the people you have hurt. Keep in mind, however, that while God never fails to forgive you, other people might. You can't control what another person does.

Confronting the Abuser

If you confront the person who abused you, you run the risk of a defensive response or complete denial. Linda, a young woman of twenty-eight, told me she went to her father and said, "Dad, I forgive you for all the times you sexually molested me." The father was embarrassed and enraged; he accused her of fabricating the whole story. This devastated Linda, and she felt worse than before.

"Let me give you a few suggestions about this," I told her. "First of all, your own healing does not depend on an admission of guilt or an apology from the offending person. Too many of us would still be crippled today if it did. You can be healed and set free from your unforgiveness without their help. In fact, I believe that more can be accomplished if you have received a certain amount of emotional healing *before* you confront the offender. The abuser should be confronted out of a forgiving heart and a longing for reconciliation. Otherwise you're not making things better; you're stirring up an old problem and holding that person responsible. This will only put the abuser on the defensive. When you go to an abusing or offending person, make sure you go humbly, not expecting *anything* in return."

I didn't go to my mother and say, "Mom, I forgive you for all the times you abandoned me in the closet, struck me in the face for reasons I couldn't understand, and called me obscene names." I did, however, attempt to confess *my* faults to my mother and ask for *her* forgiveness. I said, "Mom, I know I was a terrible teenager. I was disrespectful and hateful to you, and I'm sorry. Please forgive me."

It would have been wonderful to hear her say, "Of course I forgive you, dear. Besides, you weren't all that bad, and I wasn't the best mother. Anyway, it's all forgotten and look how wonderfully you've turned out." I didn't expect that and therefore was only mildly disappointed when she went on and on about how horrible I'd been and the many ways I'd ruined her life.

Forgiving Yourself and God

While forgiving others is crucial, forgiveness is also needed in two other areas. One is *forgiving yourself.*

Emotionally wounded people often feel guilty about not being what they think they should be. Instead of beating ourselves up for that, we need to be merciful. We have to be able to say, "Self, I forgive you for not being perfect, and I thank You, God, that You are right now making me into all that You created me to be."

Besides forgiving others and yourself, you must also check to see if you need to *forgive God*. If you've been mad at Him, say so. "God, I've been mad at You ever since my brother was killed in that accident." "God, I've been mad at You since my baby died." "God, I'm mad at You for not getting that job I prayed for." "God, I feel like You love my sister and brother more than You love me." Be honest. You won't crush God's ego. Release the hurt and let yourself cry. Tears are freeing and healing. Say, "Lord, I confess my hurt, my anger, and my hardness of heart toward You. I no longer hold that offense against You."

Remember that forgiveness is an ongoing process. That is because even when you've dealt with the past, constant infractions occur in the present. None of us gets by without having our pride wounded or being manipulated, offended, or hurt by someone. Each time that happens it leaves a scar on the soul if not confessed and dealt with before the Lord. Besides that, unforgiveness also separates you from people you love. They sense a spirit of unforgiveness, even if they can't identify it, and it makes them uncomfortable and distant.

You may be thinking, *I don't have to worry about this because I have no unforgiveness toward anyone.* But forgiveness also has to do with not being critical of others. It has to do with keeping in mind that people are often the way they are because of how life has shaped them. It has to do with remembering that God is the only one who knows the whole story, and therefore we never have the right to judge. Without forgiveness we can't release the past. Don't let unforgiveness keep you from the healing, joy, and restoration God has for you.

Prayer

Lord, help me to let go of my past so that I can move into all You have for me. I know that You make all things new. Renew my mind and soul so that I don't allow past experiences to color my life today. Show me who I need to forgive, and help me forgive them completely. Heal me of all the painful memories in my life so that I can become all You created me to be.

What the Bible Says About Releasing the Past

Do not remember the former things,
nor consider the things of old. Behold,
I will do a new thing; now it shall spring
forth; shall you not know it?

—*Isaiah 43:18–19*

Therefore, if anyone is in Christ, he is a new
creation; old things have passed away;
behold, all things have become new.

—*2 Corinthians 5:17*

Let all bitterness, wrath, anger, clamor,
and evil speaking be put away from you,
with all malice. And be kind to one another,
tenderhearted, forgiving one another, even as
God in Christ forgave you.

—*Ephesians 4:31–32*

He who loves his brother abides in the
light, and there is no cause for stumbling in
him. But he who hates his brother is in
darkness and walks in darkness, and does
not know where he is going, because
the darkness has blinded his eyes.

—*1 John 2:10–11*

Step Two: Live in Obedience

When will I ever get to the point where I no longer hurt inside?" I asked God in prayer one day a few months after my counseling session with Mary Anne. Even though I had been set free from depression and my life was far more stable than it had ever been, I still lived on an emotional roller coaster. My questions to God during that time went on and on:

"When will I stop feeling like a failure?"

"When will I not be devastated by what other people say to me?"

"When will I not view every hint of misfortune as the end of the world?"

"When will I be able to go through the normal occurrences of life without being traumatized by them?"

There were no answers from God at that moment, but as I read the Bible the next morning, my eyes fell on the words, "Why do you call me 'Lord, Lord,' and not do the things which I say?" (Luke 6:46). The passage went on to explain that anyone who hears the words of the Lord and does not put them into practice is building a house with no foundation. When the storm comes, it will collapse and be completely destroyed.

Could it be that I'm getting blown over and destroyed by every wind of circumstance that comes my way because I'm not doing what the Lord says to do in some area? I wondered. I knew I had laid a strong foundation by giving my life to the Lord, but it appeared that this foundation could only be stabilized and protected through my obedience.

I searched the Bible for more information, and every place I turned I read more about the rewards of obeying God, passages like "Blessed are those who hear the word of God and keep it!"(Luke 11:28).

And the more I read, the more I saw the link between *obedience* and the *presence of God*. "If anyone loves Me he will keep My word; and My Father will love him, and We will come to him and make Our home with him" (John 14:23). By this time I was convinced that I could only find wholeness and restoration in His presence, so the promise that my obedience would open the door to God's dwelling with me was particularly impressive.

I also saw a definite connection between *obedience* and the *love of God*. "If anyone obeys His Word, God's love is truly made complete in him" (1 John 2:5 NIV). According to the Bible, God doesn't stop loving us if we *don't* obey. Even if He doesn't love the way we live, He still loves *us*. But we are unable to feel or enjoy that love fully if we're not living as God intended us to live.

The more I read about obedience, the more I realized that my disobedience of God's directives could explain why nothing happened when I prayed the same prayers over and over. The Bible says, "One who turns away his ear from hearing the law, even his prayer is an abomination" (Prov. 28:9).

If I'm not obeying God in some way, then I shouldn't expect to get my prayers answered, I thought.

For anyone who has been emotionally wounded in any way, a certain amount of deliverance and healing will happen in your life just because you are obedient to God. The Bible says, "He who obeys instructions guards his life" (Prov. 19:16 NIV). The more obedient you are, the more bondage will be stripped away from your life. There is also a certain healthy confidence that comes from knowing you've obeyed God. This confidence builds self-worth and nourishes a broken personality. You start the process by being willing to say:

> God, I don't want to be someone who collapses every time something shakes me. I don't want anything to separate me from Your presence and love. And I really do have a heart that wants to obey. Please show me where I am not living in obedience, and help me to do what I need to do.

There are many different areas of obedience, but the ones I will mention in this chapter are important for emotional health. Just take one step at a time, remembering that the power of the Holy Spirit in us enables us to obey God.

It took me years to figure out I was supposed to be doing these things, and I still review them regularly to see where I've gotten off the mark. I hope you will move into them more quickly than I did and begin to enjoy the benefits sooner.

Live in Obedience by Taking Charge of Your Mind

"I've started having uncontrollably bizarre and frightening thoughts," I told Mary Anne some time after my deliverance in her office. "I've been doing so well, I don't know what happened. Sometimes I feel like I'm losing my mind. It's scary. I've always been afraid I'd go crazy like my mother."

"Let me assure you that you are not going to go crazy like your mother," she said with great confidence. "First of all, you are not your mother. You are a different person. Second, you are not mentally ill. But you *are* being mentally oppressed."

"What do you mean?" I asked.

"The Bible tells us we have the mind of Christ when we are born again, but we still have to allow this mind to be in us," Mary Anne explained. "You've been delivered from major oppression, but you still must choose to let the mind of Christ control you. You've started allowing yourself to listen to whatever thoughts come into your mind."

This was new information to me. I knew that God gives us a choice about how we live, but I had never realized that I could choose my thoughts. I grew up with a mother whose every wild thought controlled her. From that I had determined that we must all be victims of our minds.

"The Bible makes it clear we are not to conform to the world's way of thinking," Mary Anne continued. "It says we are to renew our minds by taking 'captive every thought to make it obedient to Christ' (2 Cor. 10:5 NIV). God has also made clear what we *are* to allow into our minds. 'Whatever is *true*, whatever is *noble*, whatever is *right*, whatever is *pure*, whatever is *lovely*, whatever is *admirable*—if anything is *excellent* or *praiseworthy*—-think about such things' (Phil. 4:8 NIV, emphasis added). God is very specific about this, and *you* need to be too."

"But what about tormenting sexual thoughts?" I asked. "I'll be sitting in church and suddenly the most perverse sexual image flashes across my mind."

"Let me ask you something," she answered. "Do you choose to think these vile sexual thoughts?"

"Definitely not!" I responded immediately.

"So where do they come from?"

"Not God," I said with great certainty.

"Of course not. They come from the enemy of your soul. Satan puts those thoughts there, and you've accepted them as yours. That's why you feel guilty about them. This is mental oppression, a ploy of the devil. When he starts to bring up things like that, you have to tell him to leave you alone."

"You mean if I resist the thoughts, they will leave?"

"Yes, eventually," Mary Anne assured me.

"Well, what about horrendously frightening thoughts? Last night quite unexpectedly I envisioned in vivid detail an airplane suddenly crashing into our house, exploding in flames and burning my children to death. I could hardly sleep because of it."

"Everyone has fear at one time or another," she said. "But is there any particular reason you should fear disaster coming upon your children?"

"No, not really."

"Would you *choose* to be afraid?"

"Never!"

"Of course you wouldn't. So where do fears come from? They are from the evil one. Recognize that and don't take fear upon you. Satan has bound people in the areas of lust and fear more than any other."

What a revelation! Suddenly all my tormenting thoughts didn't seem so overpowering. Nor did I have to feel guilty about them, now that I was certain they were not coming from me. All I had to do was resist them in Jesus' name.

Immediately I set about doing just that. Whenever upsetting thoughts came into my mind and I identified them as not from me or God, I said aloud, "I will not be controlled by negative thoughts. I renounce these sexual images in the name of Jesus. I reject visions of disaster coming upon me and my family. I refuse the suggestion that I will go crazy like my mother. God has not given me a spirit of fear. He has given me a sound mind. I have the mind of Christ and I refuse any thoughts that are not of the Lord."

Although sometimes I had to pray like that for days, relief usually came right away when I resisted negative mental suggestions and spent much time praising God. I did the same thing whenever a memory of a past incident played itself over and over in my mind like a stuck record. "I give that memory to You, Jesus, and I refuse to think about it anymore," I said every time it came to mind. That always stopped it. Now, even though I can be as vulnerable to an attack of mental oppression as anyone, I quickly identify it and refuse to give place to it.

I'm convinced that we can never be totally healed of emotional damage when a war is constantly going on in our minds—especially if we are losing the battle. The Bible says not to "walk as the rest of the Gentiles walk, in the futility of their mind, having their understanding darkened, being alienated from the life of God, because of the ignorance that is in them" (Eph. 4:17–18). We have to choose daily to allow the mind of Christ to be in us and the wisdom of God to guide us.

What Is Your State of Mind?

Considering that the state of your mind affects the state of your heart, which in turn affects your entire being, it's wise to evaluate the condition of your mind frequently by asking yourself these questions:

- Do my thoughts make me feel sad, depressed, lonely, or hopeless?

- Do my thoughts cause me to be angry, bitter, or unforgiving?

- Do my thoughts cause me to feel self-hatred and self-doubt?

- Do my thoughts bring feelings of anxiety or fear?

- Do my thoughts constantly rehearse negative memories?

- Do my thoughts become dominated by immoral sexual images?

- Do my thoughts make me feel unclean or sickened?

- Do my thoughts cause me to feel anything other than peace and well-being?

If you answered yes to any of these questions, you are living with needless torment, and it's time to take charge of your mind. Don't think you're alone, however. Anyone who has ever suffered from traumatic emotional hurts is highly susceptible to these feelings. Not only do we have bad memories to deal with, but the devil delights in taking the painful events of our past and sowing them as seeds of negativity in the mind.

The best way to control your thoughts is to control outside influences. Did you know that you can become fearful and anxious simply from watching the wrong TV shows, even when they don't seem upsetting at the time? Think about it. How many shows have you watched and gone away feeling uplifted, hopeful, energetic, full of love, and motivated to do good things? Not many, I'm sure. Usually we feel exhausted, empty, restless, uneasy, unclean, or fearful. That's because whatever goes into your mind affects your emotions. You have to be specific about what you allow into your mind and truly take *every* thought captive.

Don't just leave the television on for hours. Know exactly what program you're watching and why you're watching it. Don't allow yourself the leeway of saying, "I don't really pay attention to the TV. I just leave it on all day for company." Get in the habit of asking the Holy Spirit, "Is this good for me?" If it leaves you depressed, fearful, or frustrated, turn it off immediately. Anything that comes from God will never make you feel that way.

What kinds of magazines and books are you reading? Do they enrich your life? Or do they make you feel depressed, frustrated, unfulfilled, guilty, or dissatisfied with the life God gave you? If so, put them down. What about the movies you see or the videos you rent? Do they make you feel good about yourself, other people, and life in general? If not, walk away from them. Anything that isn't feeding you is depleting you. If it's not of God, it will make your heart numb to what is of God.

A fantasy is a series of mental images that usually involves some unfulfilled desire. Don't fall for the misconception that you can fantasize about whatever you want because it's not real. It *is* real. When it's going on in the mind, it's going on. Many people's lives are crooked because they don't think straight, so turn off any thoughts that are not inspired by the Lord.

Take the same approach when things that have happened in the past come back to your mind. Unless you are trying to remember them for the specific purpose of being healed or set free, don't let your mind play continuous reruns.

Don't let the enemy of your soul repeatedly fill you with regret and remorse over past events. Don't let your mind wander and race from one anxious and painful thought to another. Take each negative thought to the Lord immediately. Recognize that you need God's power to enable you to take charge of your mind, and ask Him to help you be rid of anything negative that has crowded in.

Tactics of War

The main weapon in mental warfare is to deliberately feed your mind on God's truth and power. Think about the greatness of the Lord. Fill your mind with His Word. Seek out Christian books and magazines. Play Christian music in your home and in your car. Put on worship music and turn it loud enough to drown out the negative voices in your mind. There are movies, music, books, and television programs that may not be saying "Jesus is Lord" but that are based on Christian principles and have a Christian spirit behind them. Seek them out. Remember that whatever goes into your mind becomes a part of you. To control your emotions, you must control your mind.

Those who have been severely abused often struggle with the feeling that they are going crazy. If there is mental illness in your family, you may fear, as I did, that it will be passed on to you or another family member. If so, you must come to the full knowledge, without any doubt, that *anything other than a sound mind does not come from God.* Mental illness does not have to be passed along from generation to generation any more than the sins of the parents have to be visited upon the children to the third and fourth generation if you have the authority of Jesus and the power of the Holy Spirit to stop them.

What the Bible Says About
Taking Charge of Your Mind

And do not be conformed to this world, but be transformed by the renewing of your mind, that you may prove what is that good and acceptable and perfect will of God.

—*Romans 12:2*

Casting down arguments and every high thing that exalts itself against the knowledge of God, bringing every thought into captivity to the obedience of Christ.

—*2 Corinthians 10:5*

You should no longer walk as the rest of the Gentiles walk, in the futility of their mind, having their understanding darkened, being alienated from the life of God, because of the ignorance that is in them, because of the hardening of their heart.

—*Ephesians 4:17–18*

To be carnally minded is death, but to be spiritually minded is life and peace.

—*Romans 8:6*

If at any time you feel confused, disoriented, or mentally fragile, say, "Thank You, Lord, that You have given me love and power and a sound mind." Then praise God until those feelings lift. If you have to say that prayer a hundred times a day, then do it. At times I said over and over, "God has given me a sound mind. God has given me a sound mind." I refused to believe the lie that I would end up like my mother. I refused to constantly replay the past and live in dread of the future.

For believers there is no holding pattern. We are either going forward or backward. We are either being renewed or consumed. We are at war, and the war is being waged against us by an enemy who wants control of our minds. If you are hurting, the evil one probably has too much access to your mind already. Don't relinquish any more territory to him. Walk in obedience by taking charge of your mind *now*.

Live in Obedience by Renouncing the Occult

"I want you to renounce all your occult involvement," Mary Anne instructed me in our second session.

My occult involvement? What's the big deal about that? I wondered. It never entered my mind that dabbling with the supernatural was anything worth confessing. I had started out slowly in the occult with Ouija boards, horoscopes, numerology, and transcendental meditation. Then I went full speed into astral projection, séances to summon the dead, hypnotism, Science of the Mind, and various Eastern religions. The occult was often frightening yet attractive. Books I read on the subject promised that these methods would help me find God and eternal peace.

Every occult practice I tried brought me an immediate

high, but soon it was followed by a major letdown. None of it offered enough substance to sustain me for very long. Even so, I was so desperate for even a temporary respite from emotional pain, unreasonable fear, and life-sucking emptiness that I delved ever deeper.

"What do you mean, renounce my occult involvement?" I asked Mary Anne. "I haven't been into the occult since I received the Lord."

"That's good, Stormie, but let me read from God's Word about the seriousness of occult involvement. The Bible says:

> There shall not be found among you anyone who . . . practices witchcraft, or a soothsayer, or one who interprets omens, or a sorcerer, or one who conjures spells, or a medium, or a spiritist, or one who calls up the dead. For all who do these things are an abomination to the LORD. (Deut. 18:10–12)

"You not only need to stop practicing these things," she continued, "but you must renounce them before God and cast out the satanic spirits behind them so they have no hold over your life." I didn't want to believe that the occult was that bad, but I did believe the Bible was God's Word. If God said it was wrong, I was willing to disconnect myself from any association with it. So I confessed and renounced all my occult involvement, and Mary Anne prayed for me to be set free from it. As she did, I felt a distinct sensation like an electrical charge pulsing through my head, throat, chest, stomach, and even my hands. Immediately I felt as if I had been released from a vise that I hadn't realized was there. I felt renewed strength, and I had a sense of peace, security, and well-being I had never known before.

Aligning with a Winner

What the Bible says about the occult is clear. If we are aligned with it, we cannot be aligned with God. Pastor Jack Hayford says, "The occult is real in its power but wrong in its source. It derives its power from the realm of darkness." On the subject of astrology he says, "The danger of astrology is beyond a simple, superstitious misuse of time. Paying the trade of occult practices is to traffic with the demonic. It isn't the result of some cosmic influence radiating from the stars but a hellish one emanating from Satan himself, who has found but one more way to steal, to kill, and to destroy."

People have often told me, "But these things are real. I had my fortune told once, and it all came true."

Yes, these things are real and people can sometimes predict accurately, but the power behind it can never know *all* the truth, and it doesn't know the mind of God. Satan has certain supernatural powers, but his wisdom is limited and he is a loser. God, on the other hand, is all-knowing and all-powerful. He allows us to choose whom we will serve, and when we decide to come to Him alone for everything we need, we are guaranteed to be winners. We can't afford to align ourselves with a loser.

You may think that reading your horoscope and checking on someone's astrological sign is harmless, that a Ouija board is merely a parlor game, or that transcendental meditation gives you a more peaceful day or palm reading is fun, but you're being deceived. It's not harmless; it's destructive. Each experience will contribute to your ultimate depression, fear, and confusion. If it's going to stand in the way of your unlimited blessing, healing, deliverance, and wholeness, why would you want it?

Mysticism won't fulfill its promise. You can sit in a lotus

What the Bible Says About Renouncing the Occult

Let now the astrologers, the stargazers,
And the monthly prognosticators
Stand up and save you
From what shall come upon you.
Behold, they shall be as stubble,
The fire shall burn them;
They shall not deliver themselves
From the power of the flame;
It shall not be a coal to be warmed by,
Nor a fire to sit before!

—Isaiah 47:13–14

And when they say to you, "Seek those who
are mediums and wizards, who whisper and
mutter," should not a people seek their
God? Should they seek the dead on behalf
of the living?

—Isaiah 8:19

I give you the authority . . . over all the
power of the enemy, and nothing shall by
any means hurt you.

—Luke 10:19

position till you're one hundred and never escape the curse on your life. You can have your palm read a thousand times, and you still won't find the deliverance you need. You can follow your astrological chart every day and never be free of your deep feelings of low self-worth. You can channel to ancient gurus and have out-of-body experiences until the end of your days, and you'll still have the same emotional pain in your gut.

Believe me. I know. I've been there. I have tried them all. They don't work. But the danger is not that they don't work. The danger is that they work just enough to make you think they do work, and they suck you in. The danger is that the power behind them is real and intends to destroy you. Even though you may be just playing around, the devil isn't. If you link yourself with the spirit of witchcraft, you may find out that you will someday have a new job and a tall dark stranger in your life. But that's hardly worth ending up on the road to hell.

Act Immediately

If you are involved in the occult now or have had any occult involvement, you must renounce it all before God. You can't be aligned with Satan and expect God to set you free. Say to God, "I confess my involvement with spirits other than the Spirit of God." Then name each type of occult practice with which you have had dealings. "I renounce astrology, I renounce fortune telling, I renounce Ouija boards, I renounce reincarnation, I renounce séances, I renounce numerology, I renounce tealeaf reading, I renounce horoscopes, I renounce automatic writing, I renounce sorcery, I renounce hypnotism, I renounce yoga, I renounce astral projection, I renounce satanism, I renounce spiritism, I renounce ESP, I renounce tarot cards, I renounce palm reading, I renounce mind control, I renounce transcendental meditation, I renounce levitation, I renounce false religions, I renounce channeling. I recognize these practices as satanic, and I bind the powers of darkness behind them. In Jesus' name, I break any hold they have had on me."

If you've been *heavily* involved in the occult, ask a pastor, a counselor, or another strong believer to pray for you to be set free from the bondage that accompanied it. Then continue to check for occult practices that can creep in.

Ask the Lord to bring to the surface anything in your life that is not of Him, and when He does, renounce it in the name of Jesus and desire to have nothing more to do with it. *Keep in mind that looking to another other than God as a source of power in your life is occult.* You can *never* find restoration as long as the occult has *any* hold on you.

Live in Obedience by Saying No to Sexual Immorality

"It's especially important to include every sexual sin you have ever committed," Mary Anne had instructed me the first time I saw her, when she asked me to go home and list my sins.

How embarrassing, I thought. My desperate need for love, approval, and closeness had been so strong that I'd fallen into one wrong relationship after another. It would be mortifying to tell her about all that.

"You don't have to go into any detail," Mary Anne added as if she knew exactly what I was thinking. "Just put down the name, confess your involvement, and ask God to restore you. We'll pray over the whole list next time."

As I left her office I immediately started remembering various instances, and each one made me cringe. I found it felt good to write it on my "sin list," confessing it to God and asking forgiveness just as she told me to do, like the release that comes from telling a bad secret. I had confessed it. God had forgiven it. As long as I didn't do it again, it was done. I felt cleansed and new. I discovered that sexual purity and responsibility contribute to a sense of well-being and cause a person to feel good about himself.

Sex As a Soul Tie

Sexual immorality is having sex with anyone to whom you are not married. People are usually sexually immoral because either they believe there is nothing wrong with sexual immorality or they are too insecure and in need of closeness, love, affirmation, and power to say no.

We all need love and, when desperate, will look for it wherever we can find it. But sex outside of marriage will never be the committed, sacrificial, unconditional love that we really need. It's not that God is a prude. Sex is His idea, after all. But He made certain guidelines for our benefit, and we can only find total fulfillment within them.

The problem with sexual immorality is that it is not just a physical encounter; it invades the soul. Sexual joining unites one person with another. When the relationship is broken, a part of the personality of each person involved is chipped away. Many such involvements cause many chips. By the time the person finds the one he's *supposed* to be with, he is so fragmented he doesn't have a whole person to offer.

Sandi had experienced many hurtful relationships and a short failed marriage with a man who left her for another woman while she was pregnant. When she came to me she was broken, hurting, fearful, and well aware of how her promiscuity had destroyed her. After several months of meeting with me, she received Jesus, gave up her drugs and occult practices, and ended her affair with the young man she was seeing. She started attending church, and within months she had shed her insomnia, her fear of being alone, her unforgiveness toward her ex-husband, and her lack of self-worth. She was on the road to restoration. I was thrilled with the way she was allowing God to work in her life.

Then one day she went on a blind date with a tall, handsome, successful young man who appeared to be everything she ever wanted in a husband. She immediately fell in love with him and, in her loneliness and desperation for affection, ignored what the Bible says about sex outside of marriage. Instead, she fell for such lies as, "We love each other . . . We're going to get married anyway . . . How will we know if we're compatible? . . . It's not hurting anyone . . . Everyone else is doing it."

The man stayed with her for little more than a year, during which time she stopped attending church, stopped reading the Bible, and stopped praying. After he left her, she became extremely fearful, depressed, and laden with guilt. She began having one serious physical problem after another, and when I next saw her, she looked old and drawn, as if she were dying. I took her back to church, where she started counseling, but it took her a while to regain the healing she forfeited. She lost years of her life and delayed finding God's restoration for her and possibly the godly husband she so earnestly desires. Don't let that happen to you.

When It Wasn't Your Fault

"I can't bear to hear anything about sexual immorality," a young woman named Caroline cried to me. "I feel irreparably dirty already, and this only makes me feel worse."

Caroline related her horror story of repeated sexual intercourse with her father from the time she was nine and of a date rape she suffered in her teens. She became promiscuous after that and felt that sexual purity was forever out of her reach. She felt an overwhelming sense of hopelessness.

"Caroline, sexual purity, like virginity, is something only you can give away. It's not something that can be taken from you. That's because sexual purity is a matter of the heart. Someone may forcibly penetrate your body, but they can't penetrate your heart, soul, and spirit."

"But you don't understand," Caroline sobbed. "I didn't try to fight off my father. I didn't even try to stop the date rape. I allowed myself to be promiscuous. Don't you see? I let it all happen."

"Tell me why you didn't fight them off or try to stop them, Caroline," I said, knowing what her answer would be.

"I was afraid to fight," she explained, her voice full of self-loathing and remorse.

"Caroline, let me explain something," I said. "You became afraid to fight the moment your own father forced himself upon you sexually. When someone is sexually abused as a child, her ability to make sound decisions is taken from her. Everything she does from that point on is for survival, or the opposite, self-destruction. From that first moment of unredeemed and unhealed sexual abuse, you were rendered incapable of doing anything different from what you did. There were no choices for you, only the illusion of choice. But God makes all things new, and that means the moment you let Jesus into your heart, give God all of your past, and commit to walking in sexual purity, you are as pure as anyone can be. Confession, forgiveness, deliverance, and the Lord's healing love are the processes that will cleanse you from the residue of what occurred in the past. Don't let the devil take that away from you by making you feel unclean."

Wounds as deep as Caroline's are not healed overnight. It has taken a lot of prayer, counseling, and love. But hope was ignited in her when she caught the vision of herself as pure.

If you feel tainted by sexual impurity because of acts that were not your choice, God wants you to be released from the burden of them. Speak to the Lord about all that has happened. Every incident of your memory needs to be spoken out to Him so that it loses its power to torment you. Then ask Him to cleanse you from every effect of it.

Building a Relationship That Lasts

Sex should only be associated with a relationship that is lasting, and without marriage you are not committed to anything lasting, only to lasting as long as it feels good. And we will always pay a steep price when we buy into the "whatever feels good, do it" philosophy. On the other hand, we gain in depth of friendship whatever we feel physical abstinence costs us. When you eliminate the physical side of a relationship, you find out what is really there. Also, you don't get destroyed when you break up. Sex before marriage means you have not established the relationship as a friendship first, and it's the very reason many relationships are not working out.

Sexual immorality scars our souls and damages our emotions more severely than any other disobedience. The road back from such devastation to the inner person is also slower because the fragmentation of the soul is deeper than any caused by other sins. The Bible says, "He who commits sexual immorality sins against his own body" (1 Cor. 6:18). We will *always* pay for it, and the price will *always* be way too high.

What the Bible Says About Saying No to Sexual Immorality

The body is not for sexual immorality but
for the Lord, and the Lord for the body.

—1 Corinthians 6:13

Whoever has been born of God does not sin,
for His seed remains in him; and he cannot
sin, because he has been born of God.

—1 John 3:9

Put to death, therefore, whatever belongs to
your earthly nature: sexual immorality,
impurity, lust, evil desires and greed, which
is idolatry . . . You used to walk in these
ways . . . But now you must rid yourselves
of all such things as these.

—Colossians 3:5, 7–8 NIV

There must not be even a hint of sexual
immorality, or of any kind of impurity.

—Ephesians 5:3 NIV

For if we sin willfully after we have
received the knowledge of the truth, there
no longer remains a sacrifice for sins.

—Hebrews 10:26

I know how difficult this step of obedience is, especially for someone who is emotionally needy or who has suffered hurt, rejection, or a lack of love. The fact that someone seems to care about you and makes you feel loved and good about yourself is irresistible. Fortunately, we have a God who understands how difficult it is. That's why He put His Spirit in us to overcome temptation. All He asks is that we have a heart that says, "I want to do what's right. God, help me to do it."

If you have any unconfessed sexual sin in your past, confess it immediately. Don't fall into the trap of thinking, *How can I confess this incident as sexual failure when that person made me feel so good?* or *How can I confess something I don't want to stop doing?* or *Why should I confess something that wasn't my fault?* Sin destroys your life, whether you enjoyed it at the time or not, whether you intended to do it or not, whether it was your choice or not.

If you are now in a sexual involvement outside of marriage, you must ask the Holy Spirit to help you take the steps necessary to release you from it. Say:

Holy Spirit, take root in my personality and guide my actions according to God's ways. Open my eyes to the truth of Your Word. Help me to want to stand for what is right, and strengthen me to say no to sexual disobedience. Help me to lay down the rules for my relationships and to resist anything that is not Your best for my life.

If you fall again after you pray this prayer, don't withdraw from God. Confess it, pray again, and try harder. If you have a strong sexual addiction, you need to seek counseling. Something in your past has caused that, and God wants to heal you.

If you are already convinced that you want to live in sexual purity and you are dating someone who is pressuring you to violate that conviction, then that person's commitment level to God and to you is not what it should be, and you need to consider severing the relationship until this matter can be reconciled before the Lord. If the person truly loves you and this relationship is right, nothing will be lost and much will be gained.

Sexual immorality closes off the possibilities God has for your lasting fulfillment. Allowing it to chip life away is counterproductive when you are trying to put the pieces of your life back together. Only an inflow of God's holiness can bring wholeness. See to it that it happens to you by saying "No!" to sexual immorality and "Yes!" to God's restoration.

Live in Obedience by Cleaning Out Your House

After the deliverance counseling session, Mary Anne instructed me to spend as much time as possible reading the Word in order to fill any empty space in me with the Lord's truth. I was eager to do that, so I decided to read straight through the Bible. I had plenty of time on my hands as I was not working and my husband was very busy with his projects, so I read nearly an entire book of the Bible each day. Every page came alive with meaning, and it drew me in like the bestselling novels I used to read.

I hadn't read more than a few minutes about the rewards of obedience in Deuteronomy 7 when I came across the words of the last verse: "Do not bring a detestable thing into your house or you, like it, will be set apart for destruction" (v. 26 NIV).

Detestable thing? In my house? Do I have that, Lord? Show me if I do.

Almost before the words were out of my mouth, I thought of my sixty or seventy books on the occult, spiritism, and Eastern religions. I had stopped reading them when I received Jesus and had renounced my involvement, but I still had the books. I had noticed them briefly on one occasion, but the thought of throwing out expensive hardcover books never crossed my mind. I thought I might give them all to one of my nonbelieving friends sometime.

I was suddenly embarrassed at the hypocrisy of that thought. Now that I was a believer, I was going to give my books on worshiping other gods to my unbelieving friends? What ignorance! Those books advocated the evil that had nearly destroyed my life, yet I was willing to let them influence someone else's life. I gathered twenty to thirty shopping bags and went to my bookshelves, a woman with a mission. I looked through each of my hundreds of books and discarded the ones about the occult or with any questionable material in them.

I didn't stop there, however. The more I thought about it, the more I recognized other offensive possessions. My search-and-destroy mission soon included paintings, sculptures, wall hangings, hand-painted trays, and miscellaneous artifacts that exalted other gods. I threw out records and tapes that were negative, satanic, or questionable in any way.

By then I felt so good that I thought, *Why stop there?* I threw out all clothes that did not glorify God. My low-cut dresses, see-through blouses, and too-tight jeans were quickly discarded. I also gave away all reminders of my first marriage and old boyfriends and unhappy times.

I might sound like a fanatic on a witch-hunt, but I was compelled by a sound decision to separate myself from anything that separated me from God. I had experienced enough of

God's blessings to know that I wanted *all* He had for me. When I finished my spiritual housecleaning, I felt rejuvenated and exuberant. I sensed a spiritual and emotional breakthrough as if I had finally passed through some invisible barrier.

Since that time, I do this type of housecleaning periodically—never to the extent of this first experience because I'm careful not to accumulate anything "detestable." But walking with the Lord fine-tunes our discernment, and things I've never seen as harmful before are now revealed as promoting destruction.

Years later, for instance, when my son Christopher was a teenager and was having repeated nightmares, I prayed about them and felt specifically led to go directly into his room and check through his computer games. He had many, but I felt directed to pick up one that a Christian friend had loaned him for the week. There was nothing suspicious in any way on the outside, but when I checked the instructions, I found the worst satanic garbage I could imagine.

When my son came home from school, I showed him the instruction booklet. I explained that I felt his nightmares were associated with the game. He agreed that he didn't want it anymore, so we destroyed it immediately, and he and my husband and I prayed over his room. The nightmares stopped. Coincidence? I don't think so.

Discerning the Negative

There comes a point in everyone's walk with Jesus when it's time to do some housecleaning. Some things you need to be rid of will be obvious. Anything depicting sexual immorality, occult practices, or any kind of evil, for example, is clearly marked for the trash barrel. Other things may not be harmful in themselves but can be destructive for you because of a negative association. For example, gifts from a

What the Bible Says About Cleaning Out Your House

Let us purify ourselves from everything
that contaminates body and spirit,
perfecting holiness out of
reverence for God.

—2 Corinthians 7:1 NIV

I will set nothing wicked before my eyes.

—Psalm 101:3

Keep yourselves from idols.

—1 John 5:21

The curse of the LORD is on the
house of the wicked,
But He blesses the habitation of the just.

—Proverbs 3:33

I will walk within my house
with a perfect heart.

—Psalm 101:2

former boyfriend—-even if he was a great person and you had a happy relationship—-have no place in your life now if you are married. In fact, anything you possess that reminds you of people, incidents, or things that are not of the Lord (or make you react negatively with depression, anger, anxiety, or fear) must be eliminated. Give them away if they are useful to someone who has no emotional tie to them.

What about your computer? Do you have access to pornographic or other questionable sites? This information is as bad as the occult and every bit as dangerous. What we put into our minds through the Internet stays there and influences our lives, no matter how fleeting or harmless it may seem.

To gain discernment, fill your heart and mind with God's Word. Spend much time in prayer and worship. Then ask, "Lord, show me if there is anything detestable in my house." Go through your closets and cupboards. Check your walls and bookshelves. Throw out anything suspicious. Things that don't *build* you should not be part of your life.

Spiritual Cleaning

It is also a good idea to pray over your home to clean it out spiritually. Every time we've moved to a different house, we've asked a small group of believers to come over and help us pray through it. We walk the boundaries of the property and every room, praying for the peace and protection of God to reign supreme there. We ask God to bind up any hold the devil may have had on the property, and we cast out the enemy. Then we proclaim that the house and property are the Lord's.

If you have never prayed over your house, apartment, or room, then do it immediately. Don't live in a place that is not covered by the Lord. If you can, join with one or more believers to pray, and ask for these things:

- That God's peace and protection be over your home

- That nothing evil can enter it

- That any point of bondage finding a place there will be broken

You won't enjoy the peace and quality of life you desire until you clean your house thoroughly. Replace whatever you take out of your life with something of the Lord. I bought Christian books and music to replace what I threw out. I searched for God-glorifying art and clothing.

The less contact you have with what is not of God, the more of God you can have in your life, and the more you will know His love, peace, joy, healing, and wholeness.

Live in Obedience by Taking Care of Your Body

During my teens and early twenties, intense negative emotions provoked one stress-related disease after another in my physical body. I had everything from problem skin, headaches, and chronic fatigue to infections and allergies. Several months before I received the Lord, I had become so weakened that I developed sores in my mouth and could barely eat or talk. The doctor I went to for help said I had a severe vitamin B deficiency. He plunged a needle into my right hip and emptied a large syringe of vitamin B, which hurt so badly I could hardly stand up.

"I know this hurts, but you need this strong dose to help clear up those sores," the doctor told me. "I want you to come back for a shot three times a week until you're on your feet, but you've got to start taking care of yourself. You must eat right, get plenty of rest, and I advise you to get rid of

What the Bible Says About Taking Care of Your Body

I beseech you therefore, brethren, by the mercies of God, that you present your bodies a living sacrifice, holy, acceptable to God, which is your reasonable service.

—Romans 12:1

Therefore, whether you eat or drink, or whatever you do, do all to the glory of God.

—1 Corinthians 10:31

Your ears shall hear a word
behind you, saying,
"This is the way, walk in it,"
Whenever you turn to the right hand,
Or whenever you turn to the left.

—Isaiah 30:21

A sound heart is life to the body.

—Proverbs 14:30

Do you not know that you are the temple of God and that the Spirit of God dwells in you?

—1 Corinthians 3:16

whatever is causing all the stress in your life before it kills you," he added with no smile whatsoever.

I paid the bill and walked painfully out to the car with the strong taste of vitamin B still in my mouth from the shot. By the time I started the engine, the pain in my head began to subside. As I pulled out of the parking lot, I sensed some relief from the anxious knot in my stomach. Ten minutes down the freeway, I started to feel like a new person. When I pulled into my driveway, I experienced a strange and amazing sensation of hope.

I took the doctor's advice and over the next few days went back to a routine of proper eating and exercise. When I'd first come to Hollywood to work on television as a singer and dancer, I took regular dance classes and discovered the benefits of physical exercise. The emphasis on youth and appearance in that town also drew me into eating health food. But all my good efforts were not enough to sustain me under the weight of ever-building emotional stress. I had let them all go because I was exhausted from depression. But when I had vitamin B shots, I felt like a new person. I went from hopelessness to hope in twenty minutes. Granted, it wasn't lasting, and I had to return for another shot a few days later, but I did learn that physical health and emotional health are definitely connected.

We can't have good physical health without a certain amount of emotional health. Likewise, we can't have good emotional health without a certain amount of physical health. In fact, we can suffer from depression or some other negative emotion simply because of physical depletion or imbalance. If I feel discouraged, depressed, overwhelmed, or fearful, I check first to see if I have been taking proper care of my physical health. There have been times, even in recent years, when I've felt I couldn't cope with my life and all it took was a good night's sleep, eating right, and getting back on my exercise routine to turn everything around.

Greater Physical Health God's Way

No one gets away with neglecting his health. We may have temporary success, but we all eventually have to pay the price for our neglect. I know a doctor who was a practicing psychiatrist for a few years before deciding to become a nutritional specialist. He told me he realized early in his practice that people's minds and emotions were greatly affected by the condition of their bodies. He felt he could help people's emotions more on the physical side of things. Many doctors feel that most diseases are caused by mental and emotional stress. Some, like this doctor I mentioned, believe that emotional problems can be controlled through good physical health. Rather than rack your brain trying to decide which came first in your own case, just know that God made the body as well as the soul and the spirit. He expects us to take care of all three. Right alongside the steps you are taking toward emotional wholeness, you must be taking steps toward physical wholeness.

First of all, you should have regular checkups to make sure you are in good health. If you have specific physical problems, don't just let them go. Get a doctor's attention for them. Then take stock of the way you've been treating your body. This is not to make you feel guilty, because I understand how overwhelming body care can seem sometimes, especially when it is so closely associated with your emotions. But you can take certain basic steps that will have immediate benefits for you.

After I received the Lord, I studied the Bible regarding health and discovered that there is more to good health than just exercise and diet. In fact, seven important factors must be in proper

balance in order to achieve consistently good health. If I neglect to tell you even one of them, I risk leaving out an essential
factor. Below is a brief summary of the seven different areas I
presented in my book *Greater Health God's Way*. Because taking
care of your physical body is a very important step of obedience, ask God to show you any area you have neglected.

1. *Ask God to show you about the stress in your life.* Stress
is the response of your mind, emotions, and body to whatever demands are being made upon you. Emotional pain
and negative emotions are a *constant* major source of stress,
and great emotional trauma can throw your physical body
completely out of balance.

If you are experiencing rejection, hurt, unforgiveness, bitterness, anger, loneliness, or fear, then your body is carrying a load
it wasn't designed to carry. Each of these emotions is like a large
siphon draining life from you.

What determines the effect of stress on your body is not so
much what happens to you as how you respond to it. Once
you identify stress, you can do one of two things: do something to change the situation, or learn to live with it, while for-
tifying yourself physically, mentally, and spiritually to survive.

Sometimes stress is so hidden that we don't realize we're
being affected by it. Sometimes it creeps up on us. The important thing to remember is that the ultimate reaction to stress is
death. That's why we must learn to recognize stress in our lives
before it gets serious and then take specific steps to alleviate it.

2. *Ask God to show you the truth about the food you are eating.*
Are you eating too many impure or processed foods that are
depleted of essential vitamins and minerals? If so, toxic wastes
can pile up in your body, causing physical stress that interferes

with the body's functions. When you don't feed your body properly, you become physically depleted, your mind cannot process information accurately, and every decision is exhausting. Do you realize that you could be depressed right now, even feel like ending it all, because of the way you are feeding your body? We've all experienced times where a single incident can put us over the edge, while the same incident occurring at a different time may not affect us that way at all. What we eat can determine how we react to situations in our lives.

If you are suffering from an eating disorder of any kind, seek help immediately. Your changeable metabolism and out-of-control hormones will cloud any progress you make toward emotional restoration. If your eating disorder is a secret—and nearly all of them are at some time—you are carrying guilt along with it. Making food a ritual, a religion, or the center of your life causes it to become your enemy. It was never meant to be that, and you don't have to live with that kind of misery.

Try to stay away from all junk—sugar, white flour, soft drinks made with chemicals, fried foods, highly processed foods with preservatives and chemicals. Make an effort to replace the junk with foods that are as close to their natural state as possible. Fresh fruits, vegetables, whole grains, nuts, and seeds contain a good balance of vitamins, minerals, and digestive enzymes. Correct eating must become a way of life and not a last resort in the face of sickness or excess weight.

3. *Ask God to show you about exercise.* The main purpose of exercise is to keep the body healthy by enabling it to do four extremely important things: eliminate poisons, increase circulation, strengthen muscles, and eliminate stress.

Everybody ought to do some kind of regular physical exercise. Ask God specifically what *you* should be doing. It doesn't have to be an added pressure to you. It should be a relief. It doesn't need to be anything fancy either. You don't have to pay hundreds of dollars for the perfect exercise outfit, the gym membership, the equipment, or the video recorder. Those things are nice, but don't feel bad if you don't have them. The greatest exercise you can do for your body, mind, and emotions is walking. Go out for a walk every day in a safe area, even if it's only ten to fifteen minutes, and see if it doesn't positively affect your emotions.

Certain frustrations that build up body tension can be worked out in exercise. Toxic wastes and poisons that build up in your system and lower your emotional well-being will be flushed out by proper exercise. An aerobics class, twenty minutes on the treadmill, a good Christian exercise video, or a daily walk outside in the fresh air could turn your life around.

4. *Ask God to show you about drinking water.* Water is involved in every single process in our bodies, including digestion, circulation, absorption, and elimination. It is a primary transporter of nutrients through the body, and it carries poisons out of the body.

Thirst does not always adequately indicate the body's need for water, so we should make sure we drink about eight eight-ounce glasses of water a day. Use a filtering system or buy bottled water from a reputable company. It's hard to flush impurities from your system with water that has more impurities than you have.

5. *Ask God to show you about prayer and fasting.* Fasting with prayer is an important spiritual step, which I will explain later, and it is also important for your body as a natural self-healing and cleansing process. During a fast the

energy used to digest, assimilate, and metabolize is spent purifying the body.

6. *Ask God to show you about spending time daily in fresh air and natural sunlight.* Fresh air and natural light bring a certain amount of healing and rejuvenation to every part of the body and mind. Natural light is a powerful healer, germ killer, remedial agent, and relaxer. Scientists are now discovering that light has a significant effect on the immune system and the emotions. Any activity or exercise done outside increases your inhalation of fresh air, which also aids in cleansing the body of impurities.

One of the greatest things you can do outdoors is gardening. Getting your hands in the earth has a miraculous calming effect upon your whole being. Digging up weeds or planting flowers and vegetables is great therapy. You can do other things outside too—sweep off your front step, water your lawn, rake leaves, or wash windows. Anything that gets you outside for a few minutes every day is good for your emotional and physical health.

Of course, you need to be careful not to do these activities in extreme heat or cold, and you need to take precaution against exposure to UVB rays by using a good sunblock on exposed skin. Then the benefits of natural sunlight get through without the damaging effects.

7. *Ask God to show you about getting enough rest.* You need to be able to achieve a deep, sound, completely refreshing sleep naturally, without drugs. During sleep, food is transformed into tissue, the entire system is cleansed of poisons, and the body repairs itself and recuperates. Those things can only happen fully during sleep when the nervous system

slows down. Sleeping pills, alcohol, or drugs interfere with those processes. Make it your goal to experience deep, rejuvenating sleep without them.

If everything is working properly in your life, good sleep comes automatically. If it doesn't, it usually means that one or more of the other six areas of health care is out of order. Don't make any life-changing decisions when you're exhausted. A good night's sleep could change your mind—completely.

Try not to view taking care of your health as an overwhelming and complex task. It's really not. It's the way God wants us to live and it's a point of obedience. The Bible says:

> Do you not know that your body is the temple of the Holy Spirit who is in you, whom you have from God, and you are not your own? For you were bought at a price; therefore glorify God in your body and in your spirit, which are God's. (1 Cor. 6:19–20)

Take good care of God's temple.

Live in Obedience by Watching What You Say

God created the world by speaking it into existence. Since we are made in His likeness and His Spirit dwells in us, we have the power to speak our own worlds into existence too. When we constantly speak negatively about ourselves or our circumstances, we cut off the possibility of things being any different than what we've just spoken.

I spoke many negatives like "I'm a failure," "I'm ugly," "Nothing ever goes right," "Nobody really cares about me," until one day the Holy Spirit spoke to my heart through Proverbs 18:21: "Death and life are in the power of the tongue." A quick inventory of the things I had said aloud and in my mind revealed that I had been speaking death. This thought was frightening.

One clear example of my negative thinking had to do with my speech problems. I'd had them since childhood and was teased about them all through school. This may seem insignificant, but having something wrong with your speech is like having something wrong with your face. Everyone observes it and forms an immediate opinion and response to you because of it. As soon as I was old enough to work and afford professional help, I worked with a speech therapist every week. I practiced day after day, year after year, to gain what seemed to be only a little improvement.

Several years after Michael and I were married, I was asked to speak in different churches. In spite of all my hard work with the therapist, I still lost my voice about halfway through each engagement because of the tension in my neck. I became deeply discouraged and felt like a failure.

"I'll never be able to speak right," I cried time and again in despair and frustration. But as I said those words one day, the Lord spoke to my heart, saying, *You're bringing death to your situation because you're not speaking the truth about it.*

"What does that mean, Lord? Am I supposed to deny what's really happening to me?" I asked God.

Do not speak what you think to be truth or what seems to be truth, He replied to my heart, *but rather speak what you know to be the truth of my Word.*

"What does Your truth say about my speech impediment?" I questioned further. "Show me, Lord. Help me to see."

Over the next few days, certain Scriptures came to my attention. First I read Isaiah 32:4: "The stammering tongue will be fluent and clear" (NIV). Then Pastor Jack read Isaiah 51:16 during his Sunday sermon:

> I have put My words in your mouth;
> I have covered you with the shadow of My hand.

Later, when I told my prayer group about my struggle, one of the women shared Isaiah 50:4 with me:

> The LORD God has given Me
> The tongue of the learned,
> That I should know how to speak
> A word in season to him who is weary.

Okay, Lord, I get the point, I thought. *The truth of Your Word is that I can speak with intelligence, fluency, and clarity because You have put Your words in my mouth.*

After that, each time I was tempted to give in to discouragement, I spoke those Scriptures to myself and said, "Thank You, Lord, for helping me to speak slowly and clearly. I can do all things through Christ who strengthens me. I praise You, Lord, that You will give me the words to say and anoint them to have life. Thank You for my instructed tongue. Because of You I *can* speak."

I purposely cleared out other negatives from my speech. I no longer said "I'm a failure" because God's Word says the opposite is true about me. I stopped saying "I'm hopeless" and started acknowledging God as the hope of my life.

Soon after, when I was asked to speak at a large women's meeting, I took all my fears about it to the Lord in prayer and didn't let my mouth say that I was going to fail. I spoke God's truth instead of voicing my own negative opinions. As

What the Bible Says About
Watching What You Say

He who guards his mouth preserves his life, but he
who opens wide his lips shall have destruction.
—Proverbs 13:3

But I say to you that for every idle word men
may speak, they will give account
of it in the day of judgment.
—Matthew 12:36

There is one who speaks like the piercings of a
sword, but the tongue of the wise promotes health.
—Proverbs 12:18

A word fitly spoken is like apples of gold
in settings of silver.
—Proverbs 25:11

Let the words of my mouth and the meditation
of my heart be acceptable in Your sight,
O LORD, my strength and my redeemer.
—Psalm 19:14

The lips of the righteous know
what is acceptable, but the mouth of
the wicked what is perverse.
—Proverbs 10:32

a result, my talk went so well that an entire speaking ministry opened up to me. To this day, I say those Scriptures and praise God for them each time before I speak.

Look Who's Talking!

We often speak what we hear the devil saying to our minds and think it's truth: "You're such a failure. You'd be better off dead." Or we repeat to ourselves what someone else said to us years ago: "You're worthless. You'll never amount to anything." The Bible says, "You are snared by the words of your mouth" (Prov. 6:2). That includes our silent messages to ourselves as well as what we speak aloud. We can't be healed if we continually speak bondage upon ourselves and infect our own emotions. We need to learn exactly who's talking in our minds. Is it the voice of God, is it our flesh, or is it the devil?

When talking about yourself, speak words of hope, health, encouragement, life, and purpose. They are God's truth for you. Wipe words of hopelessness, doubt, and negativity from your vocabulary. I'm not talking about when you're in counseling or pouring out your heart to God or to a friend. By all means, be honest about your feelings. Giving the impression that nothing is wrong when something *is* wrong is living a lie.

But when you are speaking about the way you feel, speak God's truth along with it. Rather than saying, "Life is the pits," say, "I feel sad today, but I know God is in charge of my life and will perfect all that concerns me" (Ps. 138:8). If you can't think anything positive, say, "Lord, show me Your truth about my situation."

Check to see how you have been speaking lately by asking yourself these questions:

- Do I ever say anything negative about myself or others?

- Do I ever speak words that bring death rather than life into my situations and relationships?

- Is my first reaction to people and events influenced by dread, fear, anger, suspicion, or hopelessness, rather than calm assurance that God is in charge?

If you answered yes to any of these questions, then let that be a sign to you that your heart needs to be filled with more of the Lord. Don't even take the time to feel condemned. Go straight to God and say, "Lord, forgive me for speaking negatively. Help me to speak only words of truth and life. Give me a fresh filling of Your Holy Spirit and let it overflow through me."

Don't work against what God wants to do in you by allowing negative speech. And don't be hard on yourself. Treat yourself with respect and kindness. Say as David did, "I have resolved that my mouth will not sin" (Ps. 17:3 NIV).

Live in Obedience by Fasting and Prayer

In our first counseling session, Mary Anne suggested that I fast for three full days, drinking only water, and then return to her office with the list of sins I mentioned earlier. I did as she instructed, drinking water and praying every time I felt hungry. After the first day, the hunger pangs weren't bad. In fact, it was much easier than I had anticipated. When she called to cancel our appointment and reschedule it for the following week, I had to fast three days again.

Nothing's going to happen, I thought. *I've been depressed for twenty years, and it's never going to be any different. I was foolish to hope otherwise.*

Through the week, as my depression grew in degree and intensity, the fasting was hard and I wanted to give up, but I obeyed anyway. On the day of my counseling appointment, I prayed for a miracle, but I was really afraid to hope for one. However, from the moment I entered the counseling office something was different. My mind was clearer, but most of all I sensed the presence and power of the Lord far more profoundly than I ever had before.

The next morning, I woke up without depression. Day after day I waited for it to come back, but it didn't. In fact, even though I was depressed at times later on, it was never that intense, nor was I ever controlled by it again. I believe that fasting helped me to be set free with greater speed and completeness.

Who, Me? Why Should I Fast?

God designed fasting to bring us into a deeper knowledge of Him, to release the Holy Spirit's work in our lives, and to bring us to greater health and wholeness. Fasting blesses every area of our mental, physical, spiritual, and emotional lives. It breaks down strongholds that we are not even aware the enemy has erected against us. In fact, the Bible says certain spirits can only be broken through fasting. When Jesus' disciples asked why evil spirits didn't submit to them, He replied, "This kind can come out by nothing but prayer and fasting" (Mark 9:29).

Fasting is like getting a holy oiling so the devil can't hold on to you. It's designed

> To loose the bonds of wickedness,
> To undo the heavy burdens,
> To let the oppressed go free,
> And . . . break every yoke. (Isa. 58:6)

Even if fasting accomplished no more than that, anyone seeking emotional wholeness would certainly want to take that step of obedience.

Who doesn't desire to be free from every hold of the devil? Who doesn't need the power of God to penetrate his life and circumstances? Who doesn't want to be released from at least one negative emotion? We all do. So what's holding us back? *Ignorance and fear.* We are ignorant of what the Bible says on the subject, and of what fasting can accomplish, and of all of its wonderful benefits. We are also afraid we'll die in the night if we go to bed without dinner. Or at least we fear the hunger, headache, nausea, weakness, and dizziness that can accompany infrequent fasts. But there are many good reasons to put up with this discomfort, a number of which I list in this chapter.

There are more than eighty references to fasting in the Old *and* New Testaments. Jesus Himself fasted. If fasting were dangerous or something to fear, why would it be mentioned throughout the Bible? Why would the greatest people of biblical history have done it, and why would Jesus have fasted for forty days?

Fasting is a spiritual exercise and discipline during which you give yourself completely to prayer and close communication with God. Discipline always has its rewards. A physical discipline, like exercising, has physical rewards. A spiritual discipline, like fasting, has spiritual rewards. (Fasting has physical benefits also, but for the purpose of this book I will only emphasize the spiritual.)

You don't fast to get God to love you. He already loves you, and He will love you just as much whether you fast or not. It is also not a time to get what you want from God. It *is* a time to draw closer to Him, to sensitize your soul to His Spirit, and to see Him work mightily on your behalf.

How Should I Fast?

Once you are convinced of the rightness of fasting, you need to take the first step. Begin by simply skipping a meal, drinking water, and praying through it. Say, "God, I fast this meal to your glory and to the breaking down of strongholds in my life." Then lift up in prayer all the areas where you know you need freedom. Say, for example, "Lord, I fast this day for the breaking down of strongholds the devil has erected in my mind in the way of depression, confusion, unforgiveness, or anger."

The next time you fast, try skipping *two* meals, drinking water and praying through each one. See if you can work up to a full twenty-four- to thirty-six-hour water fast once a week. I fast about forty days a year, but I do it one day a week for forty weeks. I actually look forward to it as a time to hear God more clearly. Fasting is just like any other discipline in that if you fast regularly, it becomes easier. Also, the better you treat your body between fasts, the more pleasant the fast will be.

When you are able to do a thirty-six-hour fast without problems and are willing to try a three-day fast several times a year, then do so. If you have a physical limitation and cannot water fast, then go on a vegetable or fruit fast, denying yourself all else but vegetables or fruits for a day. Most people can do that.

If you are hesitant about fasting, read a good Christian book on the subject. My own book, *Greater Health God's Way*, has a chapter on fasting to help you move into that discipline.

The Fasting God Chooses

In Isaiah 58, God describes the benefits of fasting. He says that the purpose of fasting is to "loose the bonds of wickedness, to undo the heavy burdens, to let the oppressed go free, and that you break every yoke." There is so much more in that chapter that I recommend reading all of Isaiah 58

Twenty Reasons to Fast

1. To purify and cleanse the spirit, soul, and body
2. To receive divine guidance and revelation
3. To seek God's face and have a closer walk with Him
4. To hear God better and to understand His will more fully
5. To invite God's power to flow through you mightily
6. To establish a position of spiritual strength and dominion
7. To break any bondage on your life
8. To receive clarity of mind
9. To be freed from evil or debilitating thoughts
10. To break through depression
11. To weaken the power of the devil in your life
12. To stabilize you when life seems out of control
13. To be strengthened in your body and soul
14. To break the lusting of the flesh after anything
15. To discover gifts God has placed in you
16. To be released from heavy burdens
17. To establish a clean heart and right spirit within you
18. To be set free from negative emotions
19. To find healing
20. To gain strength for what you don't have the ability to do without God's help

each time you fast to remind yourself why you are fasting (to be free), what you are to do (give of yourself), and what your rewards are (healing, answered prayer, deliverance, protection).

Be sure to accompany your fast with prayer. Fasting without praying is just starvation. This is a time to be close to the Lord and allow Him to guide you where you need to go. Sometimes you will have the clear leading of the Holy Spirit as to why you are fasting; sometimes you won't. Whether you do or not, it's good to have a prayer focus in mind.

God calls all who are able to fast and pray——not just pastors, not just elders, not just authors or teachers, not just men and women over fifty, but all adults who acknowledge Jesus as the Son of God. Ask God what He is saying to *you* about fasting, for He *is* saying something. Remember that "no discipline seems pleasant at the time, but painful. Later on, however, it produces a harvest of righteousness and peace for those who have been trained by it" (Heb. 12:11 NIV).

Because fasting is an instrument for defeating the enemy, it's a key to deliverance and emotional wholeness. Don't neglect it. Even after you have been set free, Satan will be looking for ways to put you back into bondage. Be determined to slip through his fingers by continually walking in this step of obedience.

Prayer

Lord, show me any area in my life where I am not living in obedience to Your ways. Help me to bring every thought and action under Your control. Enable me to hear Your instructions to my heart so that I may do Your will. Lead me in Your paths of righteousness, wholeness, and peace.

What the Bible Says About Obedience

Great peace have those who love Your law,
And nothing causes them to stumble.

—Psalm 119:165

If you are willing and obedient,
You shall eat the good of the land.

—Isaiah 1:19

Do not merely listen to the word,
and so deceive yourselves.
Do what it says.

—James 1:22 NIV

Therefore, to him who knows to do good
and does not do it, to him it is sin.

—James 4:17

He who says, "I know Him," and does not
keep His commandments, is a liar, and the
truth is not in him.

—1 John 2:4

3

STEP THREE: FIND DELIVERANCE

When Mary Anne said "You need deliverance" that day in the counseling office, the words resounded in my head and immediately brought to mind red-eyed demons, green vomit, and whirlwinds. *Am I possessed?* I wondered.

Mary Anne assured me that deliverance was nothing to be afraid of but was a process of becoming all God made us to be.

"Deliverance removes all past brokenness and bondage from a person's life so the real *you* can come forth," she explained. "I'm talking about *oppression* and *not possession*. There are spirits that attach themselves to you. They can come into anyone's life through the work of the devil, who has been allowed influence and access through our own sin."

"Will I become a different person?" I asked.

"Deliverance doesn't *change* you into a different person. It *releases* you to be who you really are," she explained.

If I need deliverance from demonic bondage, am I really saved? I wondered. But Pastor Jack answered that question when he spoke to the church the following Wednesday evening. "You can't get any more saved or forgiven than you are when you come under the covenant of the blood of the cross of Jesus. Deliverance has to do with possessing the full dimensions of what Christ has for us. It has nothing to do with being demon possessed, or being destined for hell, but it has to do with being rid of residual fragments of hell from your past. Residue from the past often manipulates us. Deliverance sets us free from that."

How I longed to be free from anything that kept me from becoming all that God made me to be. I grew more eager for that to happen and less intimidated by the mystery that had formerly surrounded the word *deliverance*. I desired it more than I feared it. If Jesus couldn't liberate me from the emotional pain I lived with daily, then death was the only other way for me to finally be free of the pain I lived with every day.

Fortunately, I *was* set free of depression, fear, torment, unforgiveness, bitterness, and a lifetime of other bondage as well. I know firsthand that Jesus is the Deliverer and that deliverance is real and available to anyone who seeks it.

Nothing to Fear

Don't let the word *deliverance* frighten you or put you off. It's not scary or strange. *Deliverance is the severing of anything that holds you, other than God.* It could be a spirit of fear, of anger, of lying, of depression, or of lust. It could be a behavior you've acquired for self-defense, like compulsive overeating or a habitual withdrawal from people. Being born again delivers us from death, but we need to be delivered from dead places in our lives as well.

People often fear the subject of deliverance because they think it's bizarre, but it was a primary ministry of Jesus. Preaching, teaching, healing the sick, and casting out devils were basic to Jesus' life on earth. The Bible says numerous times that Jesus is the Deliverer.

Jesus said, "If you can believe, all things are possible to him who believes" (Mark 9:23). This is true for anything in your life, but Jesus said it in direct reference to deliverance from evil spirits. He also said, "In My name they will cast out demons" (Mark 16:17). Jesus gives us the power and authority to drive out all that is not of God. We do it in His name. He also said not to dwell on the devil but rather to keep our minds focused on the Lord and His delivering power.

Pastor Jack Hayford says, "Jesus deals just as easily with the tormented areas of our lives as with problems in the body. It was a regular part of His ministry. When people needed to be physically healed, He healed them. When they were bound and tormented, He delivered them. If demons weren't real, Jesus would have told us so."

People fear the demons or what they think might happen to them if they are delivered. But we don't have to be afraid. As terrible as demons are, their power doesn't approach the power of God. The presence of Jesus dwelling in us cannot ever be shaken, so we don't have to fear losing control. Actually, when we're in bondage, we've already lost control to Satan. Deliverance assures us that we are controlled by God.

People often don't seek deliverance because they're ignorant of what deliverance does. They fear it might change them so dramatically that they'll become unrecognizable and will forever lose themselves. Actually, the opposite is true. You will feel more like yourself than you ever have.

People also don't seek deliverance because they've been sucked into thinking their bondage is their fault. Never realizing that the real culprit is the devil, they feel they aren't eligible for deliverance or don't deserve to be free. Neither is true.

What Deliverance Really Is

All bondage comes from disobedience. Behind every sin, there is an evil spirit. When you sin, you give that spirit a foothold in your life. We can come under it through our own ignorance ("I didn't know that was wrong"), rebellion ("Even if it's wrong, I'm going to do it anyway"), irresponsibility ("I know I probably shouldn't be doing this, but it won't hurt just this once"), being victimized by the sins of others ("What he did to me was emotionally damaging and now that's why I do the things I do"), or inheriting the tendency from a parent ("I don't know why I do that—I must be just like my father").

Deliverance, then, is evicting the devil and refusing to be crippled by him. God doesn't force it on us; we have to desire it. We have to want to put away all the pain of the past, the bad habits, the negative emotions, the sin and the self-indulgence. We have to want to be free. God is committed to removing burdens from our lives, but the first step is up to us.

Although this subject makes many people think of *The Exorcist,* most of the time deliverance is not like that. Much of it is a gradual stripping away, layer by layer, little by little. God delivers you one step at a time as you are able to allow Him. In one area, such as fear, you may be set free all at once. In another, such as anger, it may be done a little at a time. It can also happen in many ways. Sometimes you will find deliverance in the presence of the Lord alone. Sometimes you will experience deliverance when you're with others who counsel and pray for you. Always it is *His* way—and in *His* timing, not ours.

Can a Christian Be Demon Possessed?

If you've received Jesus as your Savior and are filled with the Holy Spirit, then you absolutely *cannot* be demon *possessed*. When you were born again, your spirit was covered by the blood of Jesus. Satan can't touch your spirit because "He who is in you is greater than he who is in the world" (1 John 4:4). *Jesus* is in you. Evil spirits are *not* in you. However, Satan can touch your soul, and you *can* be demon *oppressed*. The torment is very real and miserable, and God wants to release your soul from it.

You are body, soul, and spirit. Your spirit is the very core of your being. Your body is the outer layer. In between those two is the soul, which is made up of your mind (what you think), your emotions (what you feel), and your will (what you decide to do). Satan can oppress your mind and emotions, influence your will, and attack your body, but if you've been born again, he cannot touch your spirit.

The real question is, have you allowed an evil spirit to express itself through you by sinning? Are there any places in your life where another power other than God's is in control?

Even though you are filled with the Holy Spirit and cannot be demon possessed, you are still responsible for your life. Spirits can only possess what is given to them. God does not overrule human will. *And you don't have to choose the will of hell for it to happen; it will happen if you are not actively choosing the will of God.*

Through confession we are forgiven of our sins immediately, but we still have to throw off the bondage that came with them. The best way to do this is to give no place to the devil. Each morning say, "Lord, fill me afresh with Your Holy Spirit this day and crowd out anything that is not of You."

Being born again does not remove a person from the possibility of satanic attack. And if our defense is weak or we haven't dealt with residue from the past, Satan can establish points of manipulation. In deliverance, God frees us from any manipulation that obstructs, binds, torments, or hinders us.

How a Person Can Be Demon Oppressed

A person can be demon oppressed:

1. *Whenever there has been direct disobedience to God's laws.* We must live the Lord's way. We can't create our own rules. When we dabble in any disobedience, the devil gets a foothold. Lying, for example, starts with one small lie. If there is no repentance, it will happen again and again and eventually can't be stopped, even when the person wishes to stop, because a lying spirit has gained control. Yielding to a wrong action until it becomes a habit one can't break brings bondage.

2. *When there are long-term negative emotions.* If you have negative emotions such as unforgiveness, guilt, fear, anger, rage, bitterness, greed, self-pity, hatred, jealousy, or any other wrong attitudes that go unconfessed and are frequently entertained in your mind, this will create bondage. The spirits behind these thoughts will attach themselves to you. For example, allowing yourself to remain bitter will give place to a spirit of bitterness. If these negative emotions are allowed to linger, they can cause sickness and infirmity. The body is not designed to carry these emotions, and it will begin to break it down under the weight of them.

3. *During times of involvement in any occult practice.* The Bible makes it very clear we are not to be involved in any occult activities, no matter how harmless they may seem.

4. *During times of tragedy or trauma.* The traumatic death of a loved one, such as a parent when you were young, or a spouse or child when you are older, can open the way for spirits of fear, grief, bitterness, anxiety, or denial to gain points of control. It's one thing to grieve; it's another to be dominated by a *spirit* of grief that you can't rise above. Bad memories of the past can create a point of bondage in you because of the negative emotions they stir up.

5. *During times of great disappointment.* This can happen to anyone, but most easily to children. For example, if a father comes home drunk and destroys a child's favorite toy, or if a parent deserts the family, this can scar the child's soul for a lifetime unless God sets the person free.

6. *By hardening the heart against God.* You may have been raised in a Christian home and faithfully followed the Lord Jesus all your life, but the moment your heart becomes hardened to the things of the Lord, you open yourself up for Satan to get a hook in you. For example, becoming so impressed with your own accomplishments that you no longer acknowledge God's power as your source opens the way for pride. And pride opens the way for bondage.

7. *By inheriting spiritual bondage.* Psychologists call this "the multigenerational chain of dependency." The Bible calls it "visiting the iniquity of the fathers on the children to the third and fourth generation" (Num. 14:18). You can

inherit spiritual bondage from your parents, grandparents, and even great-grandparents, just as you inherit eye color or the size of your nose.

For instance, doctors now acknowledge that alcoholism can be an inherited genetic tendency. And some people can inherit a family attitude. For example, certain families dismiss marital infidelity by thinking, *This is just what men do.* Another example is a person who, as a child, watched his parent display a violent temper and later, in adulthood, adopts this same approach to dealing with problems.

Such bondage has to be broken by laying the spiritual ax of deliverance to the root of the family tree and declaring your birth into another family in which you inherit qualities from your heavenly Father. This chain of bondage is like a bullet wound that can't heal because the bullet is still buried deep inside. Deliverance removes the bullet so healing can happen.

The Flesh or the Devil?

There is a difference between bondage of the flesh and satanic bondage. Fleshly bondage has to do with my wanting to serve my own will, my own appetite, my own way, my own desires. Uncurbed fleshly bondage eventually leads to satanic bondage. Repeatedly giving in to the flesh leads to the entry of evil to establish a stronghold. We are the ones who open the door for the devil's rule in our lives. To determine whether you're dealing with fleshly bondage or satanic bondage, check to see if you're giving in to your flesh or if your flesh is being pulled against your will.

If I am drawn to pornography, I am in fleshly bondage. I can give in to the flesh and look at pornography once or twice, and I still am in fleshly bondage. If I become unrepentant and repeat the offense until I am uncontrollably drawn to it, then I have given control to the devil and the bondage is satanic.

No matter what kind of bondage you suffer, ask God to show you where you need deliverance. Then ask Jesus, the Deliverer, to deliver you and to show you what you must do. You don't need to become preoccupied with the demon or the bondage; you need only to seek the Deliverer. He'll take care of the rest.

How to Tell If You Need Deliverance

When I'm anxious or depressed, I take mental inventory of my life to see if I need deliverance. You can do that too. Check the statements below that reflect your life at this moment:

○ I have memories of past hurts and failures that never go away.

○ I can't forgive certain people who have hurt me, even though I've tried time and time again.

○ I've been involved with the occult in some way.

○ I'm addicted to or dependent on drugs or alcohol.

○ I eat whenever I feel unhappy or have an emotional need.

○ I have trouble controlling my anger.

○ I hit my spouse or children when I'm angry with them.

○ I've had an adulterous affair or sex outside of marriage.

○ I frequently tell lies.

○ I am doing everything I know to do in the Lord, and I'm still depressed.

○ I cannot forgive my parents enough to feel love and compassion for them.

○ I cannot sense God's presence in my prayer or worship time.

○ I feel empty and distant from God, even when I'm reading the Bible.

○ I don't feel I'm growing in my walk with Jesus, and I never sense a fresh flow of His Spirit when I ask for it.

○ I have trouble sustaining friendships.

○ I can't make decisions about minor matters, and even the smallest task seems too difficult.

○ I have confessed my sins, forgiven those who have hurt me, and done everything I know to do, yet I never experience breakthrough with some problems.

If you checked any of these statements, ask God for deliverance in that area. Then read on to see what step to take next.

Remember, deliverance doesn't change you; it frees the real you to emerge. You will not become super spiritual, mystical, or mysterious; you will actually be more human, more transparent and real. When the real you is covered up in bondage and distorted by brokenness, you can't see who you really are. Neither can anyone else. Some people say, "What if I don't like the real me?" Believe me, you will like the real you that God created. The real you is wonderful, witty, considerate, pure, peaceful, attractive, dynamic, positive, fulfilled, and full of purpose. I guarantee that when God is finished putting you together, you're going to like what you see. After all, you're going to be seeing His reflection.

Seven Basic Steps to Deliverance

No matter when, where, or how deliverance occurs, seven steps are common. Ignoring them may short-circuit the flow of deliverance in your life.

1. Confessing

The devil has a hook in you wherever there is unconfessed sin. The fact that you keep returning to the same sin is no excuse for not confessing. You must keep your life totally confessed before the Lord so as not to block the deliverance process.

If God shows you the work of an evil spirit in your life, repent of anything you may have done to give that spirit control. Say, "Lord, I confess that I have aligned myself with a lying spirit by not being honest. Forgive me for lying. I repent of it and ask You to help me not to do it anymore."

2. Renouncing

You can't be delivered from something you have not put out of your life. Confessing is speaking the whole truth about your sin. Renouncing is taking a firm stand against it and removing its right to stay. It's possible to renounce without confessing, and many people confess without renouncing. You have to separate yourself from all that is not of God so that you can be aligned with all that is of God. Certain keys to deliverance won't be revealed to you unless you renounce whatever is not of God.

The first step in renouncing sin is to ask God exactly what you need to be delivered from. If you're dealing with evil sprits, ask Him to show you which ones. Say, "God, give me revelation. Show me if an evil spirit is causing my fear." Then speak a Scripture from the Word of God that backs up your authority to cast out this spirit. Choose a Scripture that applies to your own life. For example, say, "God has not given [me] a spirit of fear, but of power and of love and of a sound mind" (2 Tim. 1:7). Then cast out the spirit. Speak directly to the evil spirit with confidence and boldness and the full knowledge that Jesus has given you authority to do so in His name. Be specific. Say, "I address you, spirit of fear. I will no longer entertain you. I renounce you and remove your right to stay. I say you have no power over me. I bind you in the name of Jesus Christ and in the authority He has given me. I cast you out of my life and command you to be gone."

Because the Bible says, "The yoke will be destroyed because of the anointing oil" (Isa. 10:27), it's good to have a pastor, elder, or another strong believer anoint you with oil, lay hands on you, and pray for you. If you are alone and there is absolutely no one you can call, then do it yourself. Place your hand on your heart and say, "Jesus, because You dwell in me and all of me belongs to You, You have made my hands holy." Now put a drop of oil on your finger and touch it to your forehead. Say, "Lord, I anoint myself with oil and ask You to deliver me," and name the specific area in which you want deliverance. Then praise the Lord who gives you power over the devil. Worship seals the deliverance. Every time you feel that spirit creeping up on you again, praise God that He has set you free of it. Evil spirits cannot tolerate praise to God.

3. Forgiving

Unforgiveness of any kind hinders deliverance. We have to be continually forgiving. Ask God to help you remember anyone or any incident that needs to be forgiven, even if it has nothing directly to do with the deliverance you seek. Openly face any memory that comes to mind, no matter how repulsive or painful, and bring it before the Lord so you can be released from it. Ask God to make you aware of any repressed memory that needs forgiveness.

4. Speaking

When we have been delivered from anything, our joyful proclamation cements in our minds what God has done in our souls. The Bible says, "Let the redeemed of the LORD say so, whom He has redeemed from the hand of the enemy" (Ps. 107:2). This keeps the enemy from trying to steal away what God has done. Say, "Jesus has delivered me from this, and I refuse to give place to it any more."

5. Praying

Your prayers are more effective when you fill your mind with the Word of God. Letting it penetrate your heart will increase your knowledge of the truth that can liberate you: "You shall know the truth, and the truth shall make you free" (John 8:32). The Bible also says, "Through knowledge the righteous will be delivered" (Prov. 11:9). It's easier to stand on God's promises when you know what they are.

Deliverance happens by praying to God from the depth of your being. It can be with one or more believers praying with you, or just you alone simply crying in the presence of the Lord. Psalm 34:17 says, "The righteous cry out, and the LORD hears, and delivers them out of all their troubles."

6. Praising

Worship invites God's presence, and in the presence of God deliverance happens. The Bible tells how Paul and Silas were in prison and were singing praises to God when suddenly the prison doors flew open and their chains fell off (Acts 16:26). Chains can also fall away from us in the spirit realm. When we praise the Lord, the prison doors of our lives are opened, our bonds are broken, and we are set free. Praising God opens us to the fresh filling of God's love in us, and that is always liberating and life-giving.

7. *Walking*

If you've been delivered, you have to walk like it. Refuse to be drawn back into the same error. Deliverance means severing bad habits and establishing new ones, so set your mind that you will not to be tempted back into the old ways of thinking and doing.

The devil will always try to kill the work God has done in you and destroy your hope for life ever being any different, so be ready to combat that attack by deliberately and carefully walking God's way. If you've been delivered from a spirit of lust, refuse to succumb to it again. Stay far away from anything that tempts you. And say, "I will not be tempted by you, Satan, for I have been delivered through Jesus Christ the Deliverer. You may have controlled me before, but now that spirit has been broken in my life and I have the power to withstand it. I praise God for His delivering power."

God doesn't give up on us when we fail to walk in the deliverance He has given us, but we will suffer because our wholeness is delayed.

> Many times He delivered them;
> But they rebelled against Him by their counsel,
> And were brought low for their iniquity.

Nevertheless He regarded their affliction,
When He heard their cry;
And for their sake He remembered His covenant.

(Ps. 106:43–45)

If we continually give place to Jesus *in* us, the power of the Holy Spirit flowing *through* us, and the presence of God *with* us, we will eventually find our personalities purged of the negative emotions and habits that keep us from becoming all God created us to be. God wants us to reach out and touch Him so that He can touch us with His wholeness in every part of our being.

Prayer

Lord, I pray that You will deliver me from anything that binds me. Enable me to recognize every work of the evil one in my life, and strengthen me to stand strong against it. Thank You that when I feel the death grip of my circumstances, You hear my cry for freedom and answer. Set me free from anything that keeps me from becoming all You made me to be.

What the Bible Says About Deliverance

He shall call upon Me, and I will answer
him; I will be with him in trouble;
I will deliver him and honor him.
With long life I will satisfy him,
And show him my salvation.

—*Psalm 91:15–16*

Many are the afflictions of the righteous,
But the LORD delivers him out of them all.

—*Psalm 34:19*

In my anguish I cried to the LORD,
and he answered by setting me free.

—*Psalm 118:5* NIV

I will make darkness light before them,
And crooked places straight.
These things I will do for them,
And not forsake them.

—*Isaiah 42:16*

He who trusts in his own heart is a fool,
But whoever walks wisely will be delivered.

—*Proverbs 28:26*

Step Four: Seek Total Restoration

I was elated over the birth of our first child, and I was determined to be the perfect mom. Surely that meant doing everything exactly opposite of my mother.

One night, just a few months after Christopher was born, he was crying and crying, and nothing I did for him made him stop. In fact, the harder I tried, the more he cried—until something snapped in me. I slapped him on the back and shoulder as my heart pounded, my face burned, and I could hardly breathe. I knew if I didn't get away from him, I could hurt him badly.

I gathered every bit of control I could pull together and laid my baby in his crib. Then I went to my room and fell before the Lord. While my son cried himself to sleep, I cried to God.

Lord, help me, I sobbed as I fell on my knees and buried my face in the bedspread. *There's a horrible monster inside me. You've got to take it away, God. I don't know what it is; I don't understand it. How can a mother hurt a child she loves? Please, God, whatever is wrong with me, take it away.* I stayed before the Lord for nearly an hour before I could pull myself together. Michael came home, the baby woke up, and except for my intense feelings of guilt, no damage seemed to have been done.

I was on the way to chalking up this experience to a one-time moment of weakness when several days later it happened again. The baby cried so long that I sensed feelings of rejection and rage rising up in me, just as I had a few days earlier. Again I started to hit him, but this time I realized what was happening, so I quickly put him in his crib and left the room. As before, I went into my bedroom, fell on my knees, and cried to the Lord for help.

After two more of these incidents, I finally confessed what was happening to my husband, then to Mary Anne. Both of them took it calmly, since no harm had come to the baby. I'd had enough healing and deliverance by that point to be able to remove myself from the baby when I lost control, so they felt he was safe.

"This isn't going to be solved through instant deliverance this time, Stormie," Mary Anne told me. "It will be a step-by-step process. God wants to teach you something about Himself."

Over the next few months I realized that I was a potential child abuser. It was built in from childhood because of my mother's violent abuse of me. The only way I could cope with this frightening revelation was to spend a lot of time in the Lord's presence. Each time I fell before Him in utter guilt and failure, His love came upon me like a healing balm. Each time I cried out to Him for deliverance, He faithfully set me free. Eventually I was completely freed from my anger and feelings of rejection, and I learned how powerful, how merciful, how tender, and how complete His presence is. I finally came to understand the depth of God's love toward me.

Once we've been delivered of something, we tend to think that we will never have to wrestle with that particular problem again. This is sometimes the case, but often our bondage in a specific area is so deep that we have to be set free one layer at a time. Step Four is to continue to seek total restoration in every area of your life until you find the wholeness you desire.

New Levels of Deliverance or the Same Old Bondage?

There are times after you've been delivered from a particular thing when it may seem as if the same old problem is coming back. You may feel as depressed and emotionally hurt as you ever did, if not worse, and you'll fear you're going backward. But if you've been walking with the Lord and obeying Him to the best of your ability, then you can trust that God is wanting to bring you to a deeper level of deliverance than ever before. This process may feel just as painful, if not more so, than it ever did, but the new level of freedom will be far greater than you've ever experienced.

If you sat in a dark closet all your life and suddenly hundreds of high wattage floodlights were turned on you, you would be blinded. It's the same with deliverance. Too much light all at once would be too difficult to manage. That's why deliverance often takes place a layer at a time to match your growth in the Lord.

Being born again doesn't remove you from spiritual oppression, satanic attack, and emotional conflict. And being delivered once doesn't mean you never need deliverance again. In fact, the devil will keep trying to gain back a point of control in your life. You can count on that.

Because deliverance is often ongoing and done in layers, total deliverance doesn't happen overnight. God is the only one who knows which layer should come off first and when it should happen. For example, a person may not find total deliverance from an eating disorder today but might be delivered from a layer of unforgiveness toward a parent. God always wants you to be delivered from *something* right now. No matter how He does it or how long it takes, you must trust that His timing is perfect. He knows when you're ready for the next step. It may not be exactly the way you want it at the moment, but there is always deliverance available to *us* anytime we make ourselves available to *it*. We must sustain a spirit of grateful dependence upon Him and be willing to say as David did, "You are my God. My times are in Your hand; deliver me from the hand of my enemies" (Ps. 31:14–15).

When you find yourself frustrated, check to see that you are not holding back the process because you are walking in disobedience. If you are clear on this and you are seeking God for an end to your problem, then something *is* happening. It must happen in the spirit realm first before it manifests itself in the physical.

Sometimes God nudges us into a time of deliverance when we feel we're not ready. We like the way things have been going and we don't want any changes. We're comfortable where we are, misery and all. But God says, "No, I love you too much to let you stay the way you are. We're moving on. You're going to grow up now and put aside childish things. I'm bringing you to a time of deliverance in this specific area of your life." When that happens, resisting His working in your life will only prolong the agony. You may be able to delay the process, but your misery will increase.

Each deliverance God works in your life will set up more

healing and deliverance for you in the future. One builds upon another until freedom and wholeness become a way of life. None of my deliverances have been alike except for the fact that Jesus the Deliverer has attended every one. They have been similar in some ways but never exactly the same.

My first major deliverance (from depression) came in a counseling office after three days of fasting and prayer. My next experience with major deliverance (from child abuse) happened over a period of time as I sought the presence of God. I found deliverance from a spirit of fear as I took simple steps of obedience. I was delivered from self-sufficiency as I sat in church listening to the teaching of God's Word on grace. I experienced deliverance from a hardness of heart as I worshiped God with other believers in church. I received deliverance from emotional torment as I cried out to God in my prayer closet all alone in the middle of the night. Layer after layer of bondage has been stripped away, with no two instances identical.

I've learned not even to try to second-guess God. His ways are far above ours, and He is much too creative for our limited minds to comprehend His thoughts and actions. Even though we glimpse His ways in times spent in His presence, we can never predict how He will accomplish deliverance next. The only thing we can know for sure is that as long as we want Him to, He will continue to work deliverance in us until we go to be with Him.

Is It Possible to Find Deliverance Without a Counselor?

God would not be so unfair as to say, "There is deliverance for you, but you must find yourself a good deliverance counselor in order to get free." First of all, there aren't nearly enough deliverance counselors for all the bondage in the world, and even if there were, not everyone could get to them. God has provided a way to be free by seeking the presence of Jesus, the Deliverer. Whether you are isolated on an island, lost in the woods, or sentenced to solitary confinement, Jesus is there if you seek His presence and cry out to Him for deliverance: "Where the Spirit of the Lord is, there is liberty" (2 Cor. 3:17); and "From the LORD comes deliverance" (Ps. 3:8 NIV). In these two promises alone, God gives you reason to know there is deliverance for you whether you find a deliverance counselor or not.

Finding deliverance by being in the Lord's presence does not mean seeking His presence for five minutes and then doing your own thing. It means remaining in His presence *all* the time. It means deciding you will walk in the spirit and not in the flesh.

Walking in the spirit means saying with conviction, "I don't want what the devil wants; I want what God wants." It means facing the hell in your life and knowing every part of *you* wants nothing to do with *it* because "those who live according to the flesh set their minds on the things of the flesh, but those who live according to the Spirit, the things of the Spirit" (Rom. 8:5). Walking in the Spirit means focusing on Jesus and choosing to live God's way. When you do that, ongoing deliverance and freedom are yours.

Counselors for His People

When all the praying and seeking God for deliverance is to no avail and nothing changes, that's when you need to seek counseling. A counselor who has discernment and revelation from God can identify the source of your problem and give you the truth of God that will set you free: "Where there is no counsel, the people fall; but in the multitude of counselors there is safety" (Prov. 11:14).

This is not only a case for counseling but also for seeing more than one counselor in your lifetime. But God wants you to seek *His* counselors because He wants you to know *His* counsel. Psalm 1:1 says, "Blessed is the man who walks not in the counsel of the ungodly." Your counselor must be lined up with God's Word and God's law.

Only a counselor who has been born into the kingdom of God through Jesus and who is counseled by the Holy Spirit can help you find total restoration. I'm not critical of unbelieving psychologists and psychiatrists; I thank God for all the good they do. But I know that even *they* become frustrated. Mental hospitals and jails are full of the testimony of that frustration.

The Holy Spirit is the greatest psychiatrist you will ever find. Jesus said, "And I will ask the Father, and he will give you another Counselor to be with you forever—the Spirit of truth" (John 14:16–17 NIV). Spiritual problems will not subside until they are addressed in the spirit realm. Only counselors who know *the* Counselor can help you do that.

Even Christian counselors need to be qualified and highly recommended. I have seen terrible damage, discouragement, and defeat from bad counseling. Girls who were sexually molested by their fathers as children have been told by counselors that they were at fault: "You were raped because you wanted to be. You let your dad do it because you enjoyed it. You need to take responsibility for your actions." Such counsel, which really makes the child responsible for parental actions, is devastating.

I have also heard of far too many incidents in which a woman in counseling has been seduced by her counselor. When a self-serving man who calls himself a counselor abuses the vulnerability of an emotionally damaged woman, the consequences are devastating. That's why I'm asking you to see a Christian counselor who is submitted to a church body and strictly follows biblical principles. You can't be shown how to walk in the ways of God and stand strong in the freedom Christ gives you when you are receiving counsel from someone who is not able to do those things himself.

A good Christian counselor will also have discernment. Often we need someone with a discerning spirit who will recognize the bondage that we are unable to see. It takes no particular gift to be able to point out what's wrong with someone, but it does take a real gift to discern the *root* of the problem and know how to put a spiritual ax to it. It's easy to say to an alcoholic, "You need to stop drinking," but God will reveal to a person with a discerning spirit that the root of the problem is a spirit of rejection, rooted in an abusive childhood. The drinking is only the symptom.

Not long after Michael and I were married, we went to marriage counselors (a husband and wife team) for help. We had been struggling with negative emotions from our individual pasts, and our undeveloped coping skills made our relationship shaky. Though not Christians, the counselors had been highly recommended by some acquaintances who were. These doctors ultimately advised us to get out of the marriage. We knew this was not God's will for us, so we came home and asked our church to recommend a Christian psychologist who specialized in marriage counseling.

This Christian counselor showed us that our problem was not our relationship with each other but our individual bondage. It took a Christian counselor to show Michael that his anger came from deep feelings of frustration and failure that he had suffered as a child. It took a Christian counselor to show me that my feelings and rejection as a child caused me to interpret Michael's anger and frustration as rejection of me. We might have grown into recognizing these things ourselves, but I'm sure it happened much more quickly with the help of qualified Christian counselors.

The Reluctance to Seek Counseling

Counseling doesn't carry the stigma that it used to have. It's no longer just for the mentally ill, the emotionally weak, or people who are "messed up." It's not an admission of failure or an acknowledgment that you are unstable. It's for anyone who is caught in the stressful, complex web of human interaction called life and who wants to grow into a new level of completeness. Most of us can use some good counsel at one time or another.

Some people have hurts so deep that only God knows for sure what they are. These hidden hurts grow, and the pain gets worse, not better, as we get older. When you have a cut, a Band-aid provides a protective covering, but if a wound hasn't been cleaned thoroughly, it can fester a long time until the infection surfaces. When you are emotionally wounded, you need more than a mental Band-aid; you need the light of God's Word penetrating like a laser beam to that hurt area and cleansing so that it can heal. A Christian counselor can help that to happen.

Many of us are afraid of what others will think if they find out we are in counseling, but people respond to the type of person you are and the fruit of your life, not how many counselors you've seen. Be released in the knowledge that seeking good Christian counseling is not only beneficial but scripturally right. Proverbs 19:20–21 tells us,

> Listen to counsel and receive instruction,
> That you may be wise in your latter days.
> There are many plans in a man's heart,
> Nevertheless the LORD's counsel—that will stand.

Some people don't seek counseling because they feel it would take a miracle to change things and they are sure that God doesn't do miracles today. But God says He doesn't change. He is the same yesterday, today, and tomorrow. Why would He have done miracles for thousands of years and stop now? I know from experience that God does miracles and I firmly believe that He can do a miracle in your life today.

Call on God First

Always call on God *before* calling a counselor. In fact, before you make an appointment with any counselor, try spending one hour each day for a week alone with God, and then see if you still need the counseling. You may be surprised at what prayer accomplishes. Even if you don't see the results you need, it will certainly better prepare you to receive what the Lord and a counselor have to say.

And always weigh what the counselor says against the Word of God; if it holds up, then follow his or her instructions. If you are asked to attend church regularly, read the

Bible an hour a day, and stop seeing that married man, then do these things.

Hearing His counsel and refusing to abide by it is a serious offense. The Bible describes people who wouldn't listen to God's counsel as:

> Those who sat in darkness and in the shadow of death,
> Bound in affliction and irons—
> Because they rebelled against the words of God,
> And despised the counsel of the Most High. (Ps. 107:10–11)

However, if your counselor recommends actions that violate God's Word, then you have the wrong person. Leave him immediately and keep searching for the right one.

If you call on God first as *the* Counselor and let Him guide you to *His* counselors, then deliverance in *His counsel* is sure.

In the movie *Back to the Future*, one small incident affected everyone's future. It's like that with deliverance. The deliverance and freedom in the Lord that you gain right now will affect your entire life and the lives of your children and their children, whether you or they realize it or not. The Bible says that every deliverance you experience, no matter how small it may seem, has far-reaching effects beyond what you can even imagine.

Sometimes deliverance is painless; you are simply released and set free. Other times, however, you find deliverance only through the deep pain of remembering and facing the point in your past where you received the bondage. Pain is part of growth and healing, so don't be surprised, discouraged, or frightened by it. Deliverance is often emotionally painful, and one of people's biggest fears is that it will be more painful than they can bear. But God has promised never to give you more than you can handle. You are safe with Him.

We can do all we know in order to be set free, but we must remember that it is the Lord who will accomplish it. Just be sure that you continue to look to Him for total restoration. And don't give up.

Prayer

Lord, I know You have a wonderful plan for my life that includes healing and restoration. Help me never to settle for less than all You have for me. Enable me to not lose heart if things happen more slowly than I would like. If my expectations are lower than Your will for me, I surrender them to You. I commit to walking step-by-step with You so that I can become all You created me to be.

What the Bible Says About
Total Restoration

We had the sentence of death in ourselves
that we should not trust in ourselves but in
God who raises the dead, who delivered us
from so great a death, and does deliver us; in
whom we trust that He will still deliver us.

—2 Corinthians 1:9—10

For Jerusalem's sake I will not rest, until her
righteousness goes forth as brightness.

—Isaiah 62:1

Sustain me according to your promise, and
I will live; do not let my hopes be dashed.
Uphold me, and I will be delivered.

—Psalm 119:116—117 NIV

In my anguish I cried to the Lord,
and he answered by setting me free.

—Psalm 118:5 NIV

And the Lord will deliver me from every
evil work and preserve me for
His heavenly kingdom.

—2 Timothy 4:18

STEP FIVE: RECEIVE GOD'S GIFTS

One year I gave my six-year-old daughter, Amanda, a small decorative box. Inside it I put a small piece of jewelry that she had been wanting for a long time.

When she unwrapped the gift and saw the box, she squealed and remarked on every detail. "Oh Mommy, this is so beautiful! Look at the pink roses and the painted ribbons, and see how tiny the gold lock is. This is the prettiest box I've ever seen."

She was about to put the box away in her room when I said, "Amanda, open it up."

"Oh, thank you, Mommy! The pearl necklace I wanted!" she squealed as she ran off to put it on.

I sat there thinking, *She would have been happy with just the pretty box.* And then I thought of how our heavenly Father gives us gifts, and often we don't unwrap them or possess all He has for us because we don't see them or we don't realize they are there for *us.*

The Opening Act

Imagine someone giving you a present wrapped in shiny paper with an exquisite bow on top. You say, "Thank you so much for the gift. The paper is beautiful, the bow is breathtaking, and I will cherish it forever." Then you put the gift on the table and let it sit unopened. How sad the giver would be after spending time, effort, and resources to give it to you.

When Michael and I were married, I became financially secure for the first time. Even though my dad had worked hard all his life, he never made much money and we always lived on the bare threads of existence. When he retired and moved to a farm in central California with my mother, his retirement didn't even cover the basic essentials. Michael and I tried to give them money periodically, but my mother wouldn't hear of it. One especially cold winter day I called them and found out they were both sick with serious chest colds. They had been freezing in their house for the past month because they didn't have enough money to buy fuel for the heater. Here I was, with more than enough money to help, and they were suffering needlessly. I immediately made arrangements for a fuel delivery, and I realized how much our heavenly Father must be grieved at our needless suffering. I, too, forget that some things are my inheritance and my birthright because of Jesus. But I don't forget for very long anymore, because I know what God's gifts are and that they are there for me. I want you to know too.

God gave us first the gift of His Son, Jesus (John 4:10) and the gift of His Holy Spirit (Acts 2:38). From those two gifts all His other gifts flow. Gifts such as righteousness (Rom. 5:17), eternal life (Rom. 6:23), prophecy (1 Cor. 13:2), and peace (John 14:27) are just a few of the many good things God gives us.

Of the countless gifts God has for us, four in particular

are crucial to your emotional healing, restoration, and continued wholeness: the gift of His love, the gift of His grace, the gift of His power, and the gift of His rest. These are gifts we can't begin to receive on our own.

Receive God's Gift of Love

A few years ago I was invited to speak to a large group of inmates at a women's prison. Afterward, I was allowed to speak privately with any of the women who wished to talk. Because I had told them my life story so transparently, each one was quite open with me. One timid, fragile-looking young woman, whom I will call Tracy, confessed what she had done to put herself behind bars. I say confessed because, although she had already been convicted of the crime, she was not required to reveal this, and I was strictly forbidden to ask why any inmate was there.

Tracy told me about being born to a mother who didn't want her, didn't like her, and frequently told her so. Her stepfather repeatedly and violently beat and raped her, holding her in contempt. She grew up desperate for love.

At fifteen she became pregnant by a teenage boy, and her enraged mother threw Tracy out of the home. The boyfriend deserted her too, and she had no other family members or friends to turn to. With government aid, she stayed alone in a tiny, one-room apartment and had her baby.

"I kept the baby because I wanted someone to love," she said with heartbreaking sincerity. But she was inexperienced and frightened and barely more than a baby herself, so she couldn't cope with her daughter's incessant crying. One night, when she couldn't deal with it any longer, the failure and rejection of a lifetime rose up in her with such force that she lost control. Grabbing a pillow, she held it over the baby's face until the crying stopped. The baby was dead.

Even though Tracy was full of remorse and despair over what she had done, she still enjoyed the profuse news media coverage of her crime. "When I was arrested and my picture appeared on the front page of the newspaper," she told me, "I felt proud because I thought, *Now I am somebody. People notice me.*"

This chilling statement appalled and shocked me, but my heart broke for Tracy as well as the baby. I knew that anyone deprived of love as a child will desperately seek it anywhere, no matter how bizarre or irrational the method. The more extreme the conditions of abuse, the more extreme the acts of desperation. When you don't feel loved, you fear you don't exist. It's indescribably frightening, and you're always searching for confirmation of your existence, even if it's a negative one.

Food for the Soul

Just as food helps us grow physically and education helps us grow mentally, it takes love for us to grow emotionally. If we aren't nurtured with love, our emotions stay immature, and we are always searching for the love we never had. But how do you ever get that love when the ones who are supposed to love you don't (or are not able to) communicate it to you?

In the flesh you try anything. At a certain level of need, any kind of attention—even negative—is better than no attention at all. We do and say things we shouldn't to gain attention, acceptance, and love from others. But in the spirit, there is another way: receiving the love of God.

I explained to Tracy that the Lord had plans for her before she was born. Her parents' sins, however, were Satan's plans.

"Tracy," I said, looking directly at her, "I'm here to tell you that in the eyes of Jesus you have *always* been somebody. You've always been important to Him. He knows all your suffering. He has seen all that's happened to you, and His Spirit grieves with yours. He never wanted all this for you, and He desires to give back everything that has been lost."

She started to cry, and I hugged her tightly. With deep despair in her eyes she sobbed, "But how can God accept me after what I've done? Isn't it too late for me now?"

"Tracy, God loves and accepts us the way we are, but He doesn't leave us that way," I said. "That's why it's never too late. No matter what we have become, when we allow Him into our lives and receive Jesus, He begins immediately to change us from the inside out. He'll take all the pieces of your life and put them together and make them count for something good. He'll free you to be the somebody He created you to be."

God's Love Shows No Favoritism

After I received Jesus, I could sense the strong presence of God's love, and I had no trouble believing that He loved everyone. Everyone *else*, that is. I had a hard time believing that He loved *me*. I could tell other people about God's love, but I couldn't receive it for myself. It took some time of walking with Him, learning about His nature, allowing Him time to answer my prayers, seeing that His Word was truth, and receiving His deliverance, before God's love really sank into my being.

If you think God couldn't love you because you're not

What the Bible Says About Receiving God's Gift of Love

Yes, I have loved you with an everlasting love;
Therefore with lovingkindness I
have drawn you. Again I will build
you, and you shall be rebuilt.

—Jeremiah 31:3–4

If anyone loves Me, he will keep My word; and
My Father will love him, and We will come to
him and make Our home with him.

—John 14:23

Who shall separate us from the love of Christ?
Shall tribulation, or distress, or persecution, or
famine, or nakedness, or peril, or sword?

—Romans 8:35

For I am persuaded that neither death nor life,
nor angels nor principalities nor powers, nor
things present nor things to come, nor height nor
depth, nor any other created thing, shall be able
to separate us from the love of God which is in
Christ Jesus our Lord.

—Romans 8:38–39

May your unfailing love be my comfort.

—Psalm 119:76 NIV

worth loving, you need to understand that He loves differently from us. You can do nothing to make Him love you more—and nothing to make Him love you less. The Bible says, "The same Lord over all is rich to *all* who call upon Him" (Rom. 10:12, emphasis added). He loves you as much as He loves me or anyone else.

"God loves you, Tracy," I explained to her that day at the prison. "And if you let Him, He will meet you right here and now and turn your whole life around."

Because Tracy sensed the love of God, she received Jesus as her Savior that morning. Several inmates and two of the guards told me later that they had never seen her cry or talk to anyone the entire three years she had been there. Something definitely touched her, and it wasn't me. Humans don't have that kind of power. Only the love of God can transform lives. I never saw Tracy again after that weekend, but I pray for her often. She was a prime example of the way a lifetime of being unnoticed and unloved takes its toll. Only the all-encompassing unconditional love of God can heal wounds of that magnitude.

Believing Is Receiving

The key to receiving God's love is deciding to believe that it is there for you and choosing to open up to it. Nothing can separate us from God's love except our own inability to receive it.

The Bible says, "The LORD's unfailing love surrounds the man who trusts in him" (Ps. 32:10 NIV). The more you say, "God, I trust Your love for me and all that You say in Your Word about me and my circumstances," the more you will experience God's love in your heart.

Receiving the gift of God's love means that we don't

have to do desperate things for approval. Nor do we have to be depressed when we don't receive love from other people exactly the way we feel we need it. When we sense God's love, it takes the pressure off relationships and frees us to be who we were made to be.

If you have doubts about God's love for you, ask Him to show it to you. Read what the Bible says about His love and choose to believe Him. The love of God is not just a feeling; it's God's Spirit. Because He *is* love, just spending time in His presence in prayer and praise causes His love to permeate your being.

If no matter what you do, you still don't feel God loves you, you probably need deliverance from some bondage. Ask Him to show you what it is and if you should seek counseling. This is too important a part of your healing and restoration to neglect.

Opening up and receiving God's love makes you more able to love others, even people for whom you have no natural affinity. Radiating love toward others is part of perfecting God's love in you. It also causes people to love *you* more. This all brings emotional healing.

God's love is always more than we expect. That's why we are brought to tears so often in His presence. They are tears of gratitude for love beyond our imagination.

Receive God's Gift of Grace

"Quick, hop in the car," I instructed Amanda, who was three at the time. "The driver in back of us wants our parking place." I tossed our bag of purchases into the back seat, shut the passenger door, and hurried to the driver's side in response to impatient honking.

Why is everyone in such a hurry today? I asked myself as I slipped behind the wheel and fastened my seat belt. I pulled out of the parking space, crossed the crowded lot, and turned right to go through the narrow, single-lane, one-way exit. Just as I was about to round the blind corner that led to the street, a car came speeding toward us. The driver had mistakenly entered the poorly marked "Exit" lane instead of the one marked "Entrance." I slammed on my brakes, as did the oncoming car. Only a fraction of an inch separated us from a head-on collision. Amanda went flying into the windshield.

In my haste I had neglected to fasten Amanda's seat belt. As I used tissues to mop up the blood coming from her mouth and nose I desperately prayed, "Oh, God, forgive me for being so negligent. Please let Amanda be okay. Please, God, let there be no damage to her. Please heal her, Lord," I feared her teeth and nose were broken, or worse, her neck and skull.

As it turned out there were no scratches or bruises and no damaged teeth, just a bloody nose and a cut on the inside of her mouth. I was totally aware of the miraculous hand of the Lord upon us and that what I deserved was not what I had received. I deserved the judgment of my failure, which is destruction. What I received instead was God's grace.

Not As We Deserve

I've spent fifteen years learning to understand what was accomplished on the cross, and it simply means that *Jesus took all that I have coming to me—pain, sickness, failure, confusion, hatred, rejection, and death—and gave me all that He had coming to Him—all His wholeness, healing, love, acceptance, peace, joy, and life.* Because of God's grace, all

What the Bible Says About Receiving God's Gift of Grace

For by grace you have been saved through
faith, and that not of yourselves;
it is the gift of God.

—Ephesians 2:8

My grace is sufficient for you, for My
strength is made perfect in weakness.

—2 Corinthians 12:9

It does not, therefore, depend on man's
desire or effort, but on God's mercy.

—Romans 9:16 NIV

He scorns the scornful,
But gives grace to the humble.

—Proverbs 3:34

Blessed are the merciful,
For they shall obtain mercy.

—Matthew 5:7

we have to do is say, "Jesus, come live in me and be Lord over my life."

In my early twenties my lifestyle was motivated by a desperate need for love. Among the disastrous by-products of this lifestyle were two abortions in less than two years. Both were ugly, frightening, and physically and emotionally traumatic (not to mention illegal at the time), yet I felt relief more than remorse about them. Only after I began to walk with the Lord and learn of His ways did I see what I had done.

When Michael and I decided to have a baby, month after month went by and I didn't get pregnant. I, who had gotten pregnant so easily before, thought surely I was being punished for the abortions.

"God, I know I don't deserve to give birth to new life after twice destroying life within me," I prayed. "I deserve to be childless. But please have mercy and help me to conceive."

He answered that prayer, and my children have been the greatest example of God's mercy and grace to me. *He gave me exactly what I did not deserve.*

God's grace is for those who live in His kingdom and who allow His kingdom to live in them. We can't receive His grace unless we receive *Him*. It's a gift that is with Him in His hand. Once we accept Him, He accepts us and refrains from punishing us as we deserve.

Grace has to do with it all being *Him*. *He* does it. Not us. Grace is always a surprise. You think it's not going to happen, and it does. Pastor Jack Hayford teaches about grace that "When the humble say, 'I don't have it and I can't get it on my own,' God says, 'I've got it and I'm going to give it to you.' That's God's grace."

The difficult part of receiving God's grace is maintaining a balance between thinking *I can do whatever I feel like doing because God's grace will cover it all,* and believing *Everything in my life—my success, my marriage, how my kids turn out, how whole I become—depends totally on what I do.* Neither extreme exemplifies grace and mercy, but people who have been emotionally damaged often fall into the latter category. They feel that if they don't achieve the perfection they think they should, they must beat themselves up for it. If we are merciless on ourselves, we have a harder time receiving mercy and showing mercy to someone else. And one of the stipulations for receiving emotional healing is showing mercy to others: "The merciful man does good for his own soul, / But he who is cruel troubles his own flesh" (Prov. 11:17).

The Lord's mercies are "new every morning" (Lam. 3:23), and so should ours be.

Receive God's Gift of Power

Late one evening shortly after our son was a year old, I had to go to the drugstore to pick up prescription medicine for his cough. I left him at home with my husband and rushed out, barely making it to the store before it closed. In fact, only a couple of cars were left in the usually full parking lot. I hurried in, made the purchase, and left the store just as they were turning out the lights. The parking lot was now empty and dim, and I felt nervous walking to my car alone. About a third of the way there, I saw a dark figure move from the shadows at the side of the building. It appeared to be a man on a bicycle and, although the bicycle lent an air of harmlessness, I quickened my pace, started praying, and readied my keys for unlocking the car door.

Jesus, help me! God protect me! I prayed silently as I continued walking deliberately. The quiet sound of the bicycle came steadily closer. Just as I was approaching the car, but not quite near enough to get into it, the figure jumped off the bicycle and grabbed me from behind. In that instant my do-or-die instinct summoned all my energy and fervently drew upon the only source of power I had.

As he grabbed me, I whirled around and said with authority that I have never before or since been able to duplicate, "Don't touch me or, in the name of Jesus, you're a dead man!" What amazed me was that I said it not as a fearful victim but as the aggressive, dominant one.

My attacker was a young man—-possibly eighteen or nineteen—-but large and strong enough to overpower me. I turned on him so fast I was able to see his expression change from aggressive to stunned. My eyes met his dead-on and nothing in me backed down.

"Someone is watching us and He will never let you get away with touching me," I said as I quickly unlocked the door and opened it without breaking eye contact.

The young man stood motionless as I got in the car, shut the door, locked it, started the engine, and pulled away.

"Thank You, Jesus! Thank You, Jesus," I said as I drove home, trying to fasten my seat belt with shaking hands. I quivered all over in amazement at two things: first, my totally vulnerable position in a large, dimly lit parking lot late at night with a male molester; and second, my ability to frighten him away by the power and authority God had given me. I could hardly believe what had happened.

Needless to say, I never tested God by going into dark parking lots alone after that, but I believe that His power manifested at that moment was a gift. And I do believe that

God was watching, and if that young man had carried out what he intended, it certainly would have brought death and destruction into *his* life as well as mine. What I spoke to him was a word from God.

Receiving Miracle Power

God's power is a gift for us to use, among other things, for the healing of our souls, and anyone wanting emotional health and restoration must have access to it. God wants you to know the "exceeding greatness of His power toward us who believe" (Eph. 1:19), so He can "strengthen you with power through his Spirit in your inner being" (Eph. 3:16 NIV). To receive His power you first have to receive Him and know who He is. You also have to know who your enemy is and be convinced that God's power is greater. Then you have to use the keys that Jesus gave us to gain access to that power. Jesus said, "I will give you the keys of the kingdom of heaven, and whatever you bind on earth will be bound in heaven, and whatever you loose on earth will be loosed in heaven" (Matt. 16:19).

The Keys of the Kingdom

Pastor Jack described the keys of the kingdom as being similar to the keys to his car. "There is very little power in the key that fits my car," he explained, "but that engine with all its power does not come to life without my key being put in the ignition. I don't have the power to go outside and get myself going sixty miles an hour, but I have access to a resource that can get me going that speed.

"Jesus said, 'I will give you the keys of the kingdom of God.' Keys mean the authority, the privilege, the access. Some things will not be turned on unless *you* turn them on. Some things will not be turned loose unless *you* turn them loose. Some things will not be set free unless *you* set them free. The key doesn't *make* the power of the engine, it *releases* the power of the engine."

Pastor Jack made the distinction that the kingdom of God means the realm of *His* rule. Our will must be submitted to His until we are completely dependent upon *His* power. As Pastor Jack says, "His keys don't fit our private kingdom. His power is unleashed upon command but not for our own personal gain."

Opening Up to God's Power

Because I know Jesus and live in obedience and submission to Him, I have access to His power through what He accomplished on the cross. Because of Him, my prayers have power. When I live His way and am submitted to Him, I have access to the keys of His kingdom. This power saved me in that dark parking lot.

If you feel powerless and weak in the face of your circumstances, then thank God that even though *you* are weak, *He* is not. He says, "My strength is made perfect in weakness" (2 Cor. 12:9). Just as Jesus was crucified in weakness and lives in all power now, the same is true for us if we come to Him in weakness. Our power comes from the Holy Spirit working in us. Jesus told His disciples, "Wait for the Promise of the Father . . . You shall receive power when the Holy Spirit has come upon you" (Acts 1:4, 8). To deny the Holy Spirit a place in your heart is to limit the power of God in your life.

Because human nature inevitably works itself back into bondage, we are always in need of a fresh flow of the Holy Spirit. Ask for one daily. Every morning say, "God, I need

What the Bible Says About Receiving God's Gift of Power

He gives power to the weak,
And to those who have no might
He increases strength.

—*Isaiah 40:29*

For though He was crucified in weakness,
yet He lives by the power of God. For we
also are weak in Him, but we shall live with
Him by the power of God toward you.

—*2 Corinthians 13:4*

He who is in you is greater than
he who is in the world.

—*1 John 4:4*

For God has not given us a spirit of fear,
but of power and of love
and of a sound mind.

—*2 Timothy 1:7*

I give you the authority to trample on
serpents and scorpions, and over all the
power of the enemy, and nothing shall
by any means hurt you.

—*Luke 10:19*

a fresh flow of Your Holy Spirit power working in me. I am weak, but You are all-powerful. Be strong in me this day." This is a powerful prayer.

Don't be a victim of your circumstances. Don't allow yourself to be tormented. Don't sit back when life seems to be falling apart. Don't live your life in terms of human energy. Let the power of God enable you to rise above the limits of your life. Use the authority that has been given you over your world, keeping in mind that the devil will always challenge that authority. Don't let him get away with it.

What good are God's keys to us if we never use them to unlock any doors to life? What good is God's power to you if you never receive and use it? Open the gift of power He has given you. Your life depends on it.

Receive God's Gift of Rest

"There is unrest in your spirit, Stormie," Mary Anne said to me one day. "I see it surface occasionally."

We had become close friends over the thirteen years since that first counseling session in her office. She had always been right in her observations of me, but this time I was not convinced.

Lord, show me if this is true. I don't see it, but is there something causing unrest in me? I prayed when I was alone.

Later that week, Mary Anne told me about a dream she had in which she felt God revealed to her that my unrest was because of unforgiveness toward my father. I rejected that idea immediately. Obviously she didn't know my father. He had never done anything bad to me.

Once I was alone, I pondered what she said and asked the

Lord if there was any truth to it. When I did, a surprising tidal wave of pain, rage, resentment, and unforgiveness toward my father poured forth. He had never once let me out of the closet, and he had not protected me from my mother's insanity. I had always felt he was never there for me. I cried longer and harder over that than I had ever cried before, and afterward I felt a giant weight had been lifted from my shoulders.

I told Mary Anne, and she prayed for me to be completely set free from that unforgiveness toward my dad. I cried again, more tears than I thought I had in me. I had always loved my dad, but that day set me free to love him more. It's amazing how we see a person quite differently once we've forgiven him.

I came to see that my hidden unforgiveness of my dad had kept me from trusting all male authority figures, including God. I always felt I needed to take care of things myself. It was a subtle, subconscious thing that didn't manifest itself in me as rebellion but rather as unrest. *I* had to be the one to make things happen, or they wouldn't happen at all.

However, after this time of deliverance I entered into a deep place of rest in the Lord such as I had never known before. It was a place that God had provided for me, but because of my own hidden sin I had not been able to receive it.

My dad is now 92 and lived with Michael and me and our children for six years before moving in with my sister. Not only was he an avid encourager of my children and an enthusiastic sports-watching companion for my husband, but he was there for me in a way that has been remarkably healing. He cooked wonderful meals for us when I got too busy to do it. He kept an eye on the children if I had to leave. He took care of many household chores that I don't like, such as cleaning out the fireplace and taking out the trash. But I don't believe this living arrangement would have worked so successfully if I hadn't been willing to forgive.

Resting in Him

Rest is "an anchor of the soul" (Heb. 6:19), which keeps us from being tossed around on the sea of circumstance. It's not just the feeling of ease we get from a vacation or the relaxation of a sound sleep at night; true rest is a place inside ourselves where we can be still and know that He is God, no matter what appears to be happening around us.

Jesus says, "Come to Me, all you who labor and are heavy laden, and I will give you rest" (Matt. 11:28). He instructs us not to allow our hearts to be troubled but to resist it by deciding to rest in Him. We must say, "God, I choose this day to enter into the rest You have for me. Show me how."

When we do that, God reveals all that stands in our way. Resting is "casting all your care upon Him, for He cares for you" (1 Peter 5:7) and learning to be content no matter what the circumstances (Phil. 4:11)—-not necessarily being delighted *with* the circumstances but being able to say, "God is in charge, I have prayed about it, He knows my need, I am obeying to the best of my knowledge. I can rest."

Sabotaging Your Own Rest

Why, then, do we have so much trouble being able to rest? Why do we resort to tranquilizers, sleeping pills, alcohol, drugs, television, or anything else to numb our minds and stop our thought processes? The Bible says rest is disturbed by sin, rebellion, and anxiety.

1. *Sin.* Sin separates us from *all* God has for us, including His rest. "But the wicked are like the troubled sea, when it cannot rest . . . 'There is no peace,' says my God, 'for the wicked'" (Isa. 57:20–21).

We are not the wicked He is talking about, but we do commit sins. We worry, we doubt, we have bitterness and unforgiveness, we don't cast our cares on the Lord, and we don't always observe times of rest.

2. *Rebellion.* We are rebellious if we refuse to do the things God is telling us to do. When our hearts turn from what we know of living the way God intended us to live, we lose our place of rest. "'They always go astray in their heart, and they have not known My ways.' So I swore in my wrath, 'They shall not enter My rest'" (Heb. 3:10–11).

3. *Anxiety.* David said it best in Psalm 55:4–6:

> My heart is severely pained within me . . .
> Fearfulness and trembling have come upon me,
> And horror has overwhelmed me.
> So I said, "Oh, that I had wings like a dove!
> For then I would fly away and be at rest."

How many times have we felt that way? We are pressed in on all sides by anguish, trouble, pain, worry, fear, and horror, and we feel that the only way to find rest is to escape. But God commands us to pray and deliberately take time to rest in Him.

God's gift is that we should have one full day of rest every week and not lose anything by doing so. This means rest for the soul as well as rest for the body—a day of vacation from our concerns, problems, deadlines, needs, obligations, and future decisions. It's spending time with Him because your "soul finds rest in God alone" (Ps. 62:1 NIV). If God Himself observed a day of rest, how can we expect to survive without it? Ask Him to remove anything that stands in the way of the gift of rest He has for you.

All God's gifts are important. Don't miss out on any of them in your life. After all, you want *everything* He has for you.

Prayer

Lord, I know that every good gift is from You, and I want all the gifts You have for me. Show me how to open up to all of them. Show me how to unwrap their full expression in my life. I know I can't live in all You have for me without them.

What the Bible Says About Receiving God's Gifts

Every good gift and every perfect gift is from above, and comes down from the Father of lights, with whom there is no variation or shadow of turning.

—James 1:17

If you then, being evil, know how to give good gifts to your children, how much more will your Father who is in heaven give good things to those who ask Him!

—Matthew 7:11

As each one has received a gift, minister it to one another, as good stewards of the manifold grace of God.

—1 Peter 4:10

But to each one of us grace was given according to the measure of Christ's gift.

—Ephesians 4:7

Earnestly desire the best gifts.

—1 Corinthians 12:31

6

STEP SIX: REJECT THE PITFALLS

*I*t's not a human being; it's just a mass of cells. The baby's soul and spirit enter his body at birth. Besides, it's my life, and I have my rights." This is the lie I believed. I was deceived, and I had little conscious guilt about taking the life of another person through abortion. But that didn't make it any less wrong or the consequences any less shattering.

Deception is walking, thinking, acting, or feeling in opposition to God's way and believing it's okay to do so. It's also believing that things are a certain way when they really aren't that way at all. Satan is the deceiver, and we are deceived when we line ourselves up with him.

In order to stay undeceived, we must hold everything in our lives up to the light of God's Word to find the truth. We can't go by what the world accepts or rejects. That will only put us on shaky ground. The deception of abortion, for example, is thinking that because it's legal, there is nothing wrong with it. But when the very existence of another person hangs in the balance, it can no longer be just a matter of *my* life, *my* rights, and *my* choice. There is someone else to consider, and not to recognize that is to be deceived indeed.

In my own particular situation, I was desperate at the time of my abortions. I attributed the ill feelings I had about them to my own embarrassment. I didn't have any concept of abortion being immoral until after I received the Lord and had the Spirit of truth living in me and my eyes were opened to *God's* truth:

> Before I formed you in the womb I knew you;
> Before you were born I sanctified you. (Jer. 1:5)

> For You formed my inward parts;
> You covered me in my mother's womb. (Ps. 139:13)

I also read medical accounts of babies surviving outside the womb as early as the fifth month of pregnancy, and of babies inside the uterus perceiving light and sound stimuli. "Babies in the womb may be able to see, hear, taste, and *feel* emotions," said John Grossman in "Born Smart" (*Health Magazine,* March 1985). I had to admit that I'd destroyed someone God had created with abilities and gifts, calling and purpose. I wept. No, I mourned. Abortion is a deception, and a pitfall awaits us when we go along with it.

Of course, God's grace means we don't pay for things as we deserve, but the effects are still there. I never heard anyone who had an abortion say, "I feel totally fulfilled and thrilled about what I've done, and I know I'm an enriched and better person because of it." Life was never the same again for me. I had added another dark secret to my already burgeoning collection, and I could not feel completely good about myself.

All evil happens by deception. The devil entices us to accept things that are in opposition to God's ways. He appeals to our flesh and clouds issues to make them appear various shades of gray. We accept the gray as just a different shade of white instead of the alteration of black.

Stepping over the Line

There is a definite dividing line between God's kingdom and Satan's, and there are people on the fringes of each kingdom. It doesn't take much to put people over the edge into Satan's territory and allow him to control a piece of their heart in the process. Even Christians. All it takes is accepting a deception like "It's my body," "It's my life," "I have my rights," "It's not hurting anyone else," or "But it feels good." Such lies lead to a little lust, a little lie, a little adultery, a little stealing, and a little murder. Yet an act is either stealing, murder, adultery, lust, and lying, or it isn't. You are either lined up with God's kingdom or with Satan's.

The evil behind the deception of abortion is a spirit of murder. This didn't mean I was going to go around murdering people because I had aligned myself with that spirit. It *did* mean that in my soul I would pay the price for my disregard for life as God made it. I would not experience life at its fullest because a death process was at work in me. And many of my actions—like drug overdoses, excessive drinking, and suicidal thoughts—were all part of that death process.

We are all susceptible to being deceived in some way. Deception is Satan's plan for our lives. But the good news is: *We don't have to listen to his lies.* We may think we must give serious credence to everything that comes into our minds, but we don't. We *do* have to examine our thoughts in the light of God's Word and see if they line up properly.

An evil spirit is always behind deception. This means that

every deception brings bondage, which can only be removed by replacing it with God's truth and living accordingly. Without the Word of God filling your mind with truth, it's very difficult to identify the lies. And without daily praying, "Lord, keep me undeceived," you can't ward off the deceiver. *The devil will use everything you don't know about God against you.*

God wants us to be free of the death grip of sin, whether we've acted in ignorance or with full knowledge and whether we feel guilty or not. When you find you've been deceived, immediately confess and repent. If you've fallen into the abortion deception, for example, say, "Lord, I confess my abortion. I won't try to make excuses for what I've done because You know my circumstances and my heart. I understand from Your Word that You know each of us from the womb. I realize now that Your plans and purposes for that person I allowed to be destroyed will never be realized. I regret my part in that, and I repent of my actions. Help me, Lord, to live Your way and make choices for life. Pour Your mercy out upon me and release me from the death penalty of this sin. In Jesus' name I pray."

After you thoroughly confess and pray, don't let the devil continue to accuse you. You have cleaned the slate with God, so be released to live in the fullness of all God has for you.

In this chapter I want to make you aware of fifteen of the most common deceptions. We can so easily be sucked into any of these that we don't even see it happening. Personally, I've been snared, or at least tempted at one time or another, by every one on the list. Hopefully this will help you identify the traps *before* you fall into them and jeopardize your healing. Don't allow any part of your being to buy into any part of these deceptions.

Reject the Pitfall of Anger

The lie we believe when we have frequent outbursts of anger is "My rights are most important, and if they are violated, I am fully justified in being angry." The deception of anger is believing we have a right to be angry at anyone but the devil. People and situations that make us angry are actually pawns Satan uses against us.

After I was healed of deep-rooted unforgiveness toward my mother, I still had to deal with recurring anger toward her because of her verbal abuse every time I was with her.

"The devil is using your mother to attack you, Stormie," Mary Anne explained when I went to her office for help. "She is a willing vessel because she is controlled by those spirits. Your war is with Satan, not her."

Learning to be angry with the devil and not my mother was extremely difficult, especially when I was in her presence. I constantly had to remind myself who my enemy *really* was, but the lines of distinction became quickly blurred. Eventually I was able to get rid of anger when I wasn't around her, but she died before I could master it when we were together. Every time I was with her, I had to confess my anger to God and ask Him to help me.

Blaming God

Often people have great anger because they are blaming God for something. This is far more common than most of us care to admit, especially for those who have been abused, neglected, or deeply disappointed by authority figures. The tendency is to think subconsciously of God as being like that abusive parent, grandparent, teacher, or boss, projecting on Him attitudes and behaviors that have nothing to do with who He really is. If your parents were mean, stern, exacting, merciless, distant, cold, uncommunicative, uncaring, passive, or powerless, you may think of God as being that way too. Such projections make us angry at God.

My husband and I have a friend who is gifted in many ways but has shut God out of His life, blaming Him for a car accident in which his sister was killed and he was injured severely enough to end his promising sports career. Fifteen years later, he is still bitterly angry about it and questions why God didn't keep it from happening. The truth is that the accident was never part of God's plan. The devil comes to destroy, and death *is* part of *his* plan. This good man continues to be frustrated and unfulfilled because he has shut God off from working powerfully in his life.

Blaming God forces us into a corner with no way out, instead of our recognizing God as the *only* way out. Blaming God produces misplaced anger that will either be channeled inward, making you sick, frustrated, and unfulfilled, or vented outward toward a spouse, child, coworker, or even a stranger. It is a no-win attitude.

If you are mad at God, the best thing to do is to be honest with Him about it. You won't hurt God's feelings; He has known about it all along anyway. Pray to Him saying, "Father I have been angry at You because of this particular situation (be specific). I have hated this and I've blamed You for it. Please forgive me and help me to be released from it. Take away my misconceptions about You and help me to know You better."

Dealing with Our Anger

The Bible doesn't say we should never get angry; it just sets two limits on our anger. First, we mustn't hurt someone

What the Bible Says About Anger

"Be angry, and do not sin": do not let the
sun go down on your wrath, nor give place
to the devil.

—*Ephesians 4:26–27*

Make no friendship with an angry man,
And with a furious man do not go,
Lest you learn his ways,
And set a snare for your soul.

—*Proverbs 22:24–25*

An angry man stirs up strife,
And a furious man abounds in transgression.

—*Proverbs 29:22*

Whoever is angry with his brother without
a cause shall be in danger of the judgment.

—*Matthew 5:22*

Do not hasten in your spirit to be angry,
For anger rests in the bosom of fools.

—*Ecclesiastes 7:9*

verbally or physically. Second, we should take it to God quickly and not carry it around inside us so that we sin.

If we find ourselves angry, we must examine the devil's part in it and deliberately direct anger at him. Taking anger out on others—a husband, a wife, a child, a friend, an authority figure, a stranger, or ourselves—is misdirecting it. We have to refuse to give Satan the opportunity to manipulate us, and this must be decided *before* the anger rises.

My husband and I agreed with Mary Anne that I should avoid being alone with my mother, because every time I was, it was extremely upsetting. So we decided that whenever we visited my parents, we would go as a family. Before we went, we prayed and bound the spirits in my mother, stopping their power to attack me. I asked God to fill me with His love for her and remind me to direct my anger at Satan. This helped immensely. I can't say I always succeeded, but at least I was able to turn the other cheek to some of her barbs.

The problem with anger, as with all the other deceptions, is that if it is not dealt with properly before the Lord, it will become a *spirit* of anger, which will control your life. If you are susceptible to sudden angry outbursts or if your anger level outweighs the offense and is repeated and uncontrollable, then you may have a spirit of anger. It can be inherited from a parent or picked up from observing parental outbursts when you were a child. Or if you were the victim of someone else's anger, your own unforgiveness or inability to release that memory can cause you to react violently now. I've found that anger usually has more to do with people's hurt than it does their hate.

The Bible says, "Let all bitterness, wrath, anger, clamor, and evil speaking be put away from you, with all malice.

And be kind to one another, tenderhearted, forgiving one another, even as God in Christ forgave you" (Eph. 4:31–32). It also says if we don't do that, we grieve the Holy Spirit.

You will never find peace, restoration, and wholeness if you nurture a spirit of anger. Every single angry outburst will be a step backward from where you want to go or be, and it will keep your prayers from being answered.

If you feel you've succumbed to the pitfall of anger, speak to the devil in a loud voice of authority, saying: "Spirit of anger, I identify your presence, and I rebuke your control in the name of Jesus. I proclaim that you have no power over me, and the only one I will be angry with is *you*. I refuse to let you take life away from me by my angry outbursts. I proclaim that Jesus is Lord over my life, and He rules my mind, soul, and spirit. Anger, be gone from me in the name of Jesus." Then praise God out loud and thank Him that He is far more powerful than any spirit of deception.

Either we vent our anger toward others, which leads to destruction, or we keep it inside, making ourselves physically sick and depressed, or we direct it rightfully at the devil. The choice is clearly ours.

Reject the Pitfall of Confusion

While writing this book, I woke up one morning, and everything seemed disjointed. I saw no purpose or future. I felt distant and hopeless about my family as if I were unconnected to them. I felt dissatisfied with everything: where I live ("It's time to move"); my marriage ("Who is this person I'm married to?"); my friendships ("Does anyone really care?"); my writing ("How can I possibly have anything to say?"). Nothing was exciting. Everything seemed pointless. I couldn't get a handle on anything.

Why am I suddenly feeling this way? Where did it come from? I asked the Lord, *I know it's not from You, God. What changed?*

I had been fine the day before. So what had happened during the night? I thought back. Both children had been invited to go out after dinner with friends for an evening's activities, prompting Michael and me to seize the opportunity to have a rare night out alone. We decided to go to a movie and glanced through the theater section of the newspaper.

"These have undesirable ratings. That one is too violent. This one is mindless. This one is filled with sexual garbage," I said as I eliminated one movie after another.

That left us with one possibility, but neither of us knew anything about it. I looked through all my reports on movies, which I collect to be informed on whether they are fit for human consumption, and found no information on this one.

"Well, it doesn't have an R rating. How bad can it be?" we concluded. At least we'd be together.

The movie was a comedy that included an adulterous affair by the lonely wife of the workaholic husband. Even though that part of it wasn't shown explicitly on the screen, I was uneasy with something so opposed to God's ways being made light of and acceptable.

Looking back, I believe that exposure to the values in that movie, even though I had not adopted them, opened the way for a spirit of confusion. Had we left the theater at the first prompting of the Lord, I'm sure I would have felt different the next day. As it was, the pure flow of the Holy Spirit I had been enjoying was tainted with the world's pollution, and my dissatisfaction with all God had given me in my life was a clear indication that it had invaded my heart.

Was it just a coincidence? Was I merely too impressionable? I don't think so. Just like the bank teller who learned to recognize counterfeit money by feeling real money day after day, I have learned to recognize counterfeit spirits by spending time in the presence of the Holy Spirit. What invaded my soul was not of the Lord; it was the spirit of confusion that permeated that movie.

Confusion is something we can fall into and think it's because there is something wrong with *us*. But it is usually because we have come under the influence of the author of confusion—Satan. While life can be complicated, if Jesus is at the helm, it will not be accompanied by confusion.

Confusion and the Worldly Perspective

Confusion is a lack of proper order, the indiscriminate mixing of dissimilar things, and being mentally mixed up. *Confusion is caused by mixing darkness with light.* It is anything out of the divine order or out of sync with God. There is every kind of confusion in the world today, because what is bad is now considered good, and what is good is disdained. Life has become bewildering, and the only thing that breaks through the confusion is the Lord's presence and the Word of His truth.

Confusion is a spirit, and it's good to recognize that. Everyone, even those who walk closely with the Lord, is susceptible to its attack. The Bible says, "God is not the author of confusion but of peace" (1 Cor. 14:33). If He is completely in charge of every area of your life, clarity, simplicity, and peace are the immediate by-products. If not, life becomes jumbled, out of order, complex, and confusing.

What the Bible Says About Confusion

Evidently some people are throwing you into confusion and are trying to pervert the gospel of Christ.

—Galatians 1:7 NIV

The one who is throwing you into confusion will pay the penalty.

—Galatians 5:10 NIV

But I fear, lest somehow, as the serpent deceived Eve by his craftiness, so your minds may be corrupted from the simplicity that is in Christ.

—2 Corinthians 11:3

Woe to those who call evil good, and good evil; who put darkness for light, and light for darkness; who put bitter for sweet, and sweet for bitter!

—Isaiah 5:20

Your eyes will see strange sights and your mind imagine confusing things.

—Proverbs 23:33 NIV

How Do I Open Myself Up to Confusion?

You don't have to go to a bad movie in order to move into confusion. Too many outside opinions, when you should be listening only to God's, will cause confusion. Opposing God's Word in any way will invite spirits of confusion to dwell in your life. The Bible says drinking alcohol brings confusion, but also imbibing in *anything* that is not of God, such as gossip, foul language, promiscuity, drugs, television, movies, and magazines tainted with worldly-mindedness will bring confusion. When we try to put elements together in our lives that don't go together we get confused. For example, we attend church, we tithe, we fast and pray, and yet we entertain a little fantasy about the cute assistant pastor or that attractive person at work.

All lust of the flesh brings confusion: "Where envy and self-seeking exist, confusion and every evil thing are there" (James 3:16). In fact, too much focus on ourselves always invites a spirit of confusion.

How Do I Get Rid of Confusion?

When confusion enters, it may cause you to make unwise or quick decisions based on a faulty frame of reference, or it can paralyze your thought processes so that you won't be able to make any decision at all. In either case, it will help to remember that *you absolutely never have to live with confusion.* Take it to God. Pray about every aspect of it. Say, "Lord, I don't want to live in confusion. I know that confusion is *not* from You. I know that power, love, and a sound mind *are* from You. I know that Your ways are simple. It is *we* who make things complex. Lord, show me Your simple truth about what I'm feeling and thinking. Show me where I have opened the door to allow confusion to enter into my life so that I may confess it before You as sin and be cleansed. I rebuke the spirit of confusion and say it has *no* power in my life. By the authority I have in Jesus Christ I command it to be gone. I praise You, Lord, and thank You for the wisdom, clarity, and simplicity that are in Christ."

After you pray that prayer, begin to worship and praise God until you are thinking clearly again. Confusion cannot coexist with God's presence. That's why worship, praise, and thanksgiving are the best weapons to dissolve it.

Your emotional health, well-being, and growth in the Lord are seriously compromised when you come under confusion. Make sure you are walking in obedience to God's ways, and ask Him to help you avoid that pitfall.

Reject the Pitfall of Criticism

The lie we secretly want to believe when we criticize others is, *I'm better than they are.* But what we really fear is, *They are better than I am.* The deception we come under is in thinking that anyone but God has the right to sit in judgment of another person.

I used to be very critical of people, mentally dissecting them to see if they were much better than I, as I feared. There was no enjoyment in it for me because I was even more critical of myself. But I read, "For with what judgment you judge, you will be judged; and with the same measure you use, it will be measured back to you" (Matt. 7:2). Judging people by my own limitations was not only limiting what God could do in my life, but it also was inviting judgment back upon myself.

Crowding Out a Critical Spirit

Those of us who have been abused as children often grow up to be judgmental and critical. Being torn down when we were young makes tearing someone else down to build ourselves up very appealing. We become unmerciful because we were not shown mercy.

Criticizing others quickly becomes a bad habit that can backfire. Constantly criticizing, even only in the mind, invites a critical spirit. When you have a spirit of criticism, your every thought and word is colored by it. You eventually become cynical and then completely unable to experience joy. Being critical of circumstances or conditions can be just as detrimental as criticizing people, because it turns you into a grumbler and complainer—the type of person people generally like to avoid. It's difficult to find the love and support you need for emotional healing when no one wants to be around you.

Criticism crowds out love in our hearts. "And though I have the gift of prophecy, and understand all mysteries and all knowledge, and though I have all faith, so that I could remove mountains, but have not love, I am nothing" (1 Cor. 13:2). Without love in our hearts, we cannot grow emotionally and we will always be at a standstill in our healing and development. But we can crowd out criticism by being constantly filled with the love of the Lord through an attitude of praise and thanksgiving toward Him.

If you've learned to be critical from childhood, you must set a monitor over your mouth and heart. Learn to recognize the unrestful and distasteful quality of a critical spirit and deliberately replace critical thoughts and words with ones that recognize the good in other people and situations

If you recognize a serious, almost compulsive tendency

What the Bible Says About Criticism

Let none of you think evil in your heart
against your neighbor.

—*Zechariah 8:17*

So speak and so do as those who will be
judged by the law of liberty. For judgment
is without mercy to the one who has shown
no mercy. Mercy triumphs over judgment.

—*James 2:12–13*

Let no corrupt word proceed out of your
mouth, but what is good for necessary
edification, that it may impart grace
to the hearers.

—*Ephesians 4:29*

He who is without sin among you, let him
throw a stone at her first.

—*John 8:7*

And above all things have fervent love for
one another, for "love will cover a
multitude of sins."

—*1 Peter 4:8*

toward criticism in yourself, pray: "Lord, I don't want a spirit of criticism to control my thoughts and my mouth. I realize that You, Lord, are the only one who knows the whole story in any situation. I don't have the right to judge others. Make me a person who shows mercy, who doesn't criticize, grumble, or complain. Thank You for Your forgiveness. Help me to extend that same forgiveness to others."

I prayed that prayer, and now God helps me see the good, or potential for greatness, in everyone. It's not that I don't recognize someone's sin. But now I realize I have no right to judge or criticize that person for it. I can pray for, confront, and speak God's Word to that person, but I can't be critical or faultfinding.

Ask God to give you a heart that is merciful toward others. Having a critical spirit can cut off avenues of blessing and keep you from becoming the whole person you desire to be.

Reject the Pitfall of Denial

My mentally ill mother believed *she* was normal and something was wrong with everyone else. She was deceived. My father knew she wasn't normal, but he didn't know what to do about it. He was afraid to seek psychiatric help for fear she would be committed for life to a mental hospital like the ones in the horror movies he had seen in his youth. Hoping she would someday miraculously "snap out of it," he chose to ignore her problem. He lived in denial.

Deception is believing a lie and not realizing you have done so. Denial, on the other hand, is knowing the truth but choosing to live as if you don't. Denial is deceiving yourself.

Cyndie, a young woman whose father frequently had sex with her but beat other family members, believed he was her ally. She had learned to deny that sex between a father and a daughter was wrong, because that was the only way she could survive in her family. She was too weak and powerless to face the truth.

It took a year of therapy for her to finally admit that her father had failed her and the relationship was sinful. This opened the way for her to forgive her father, which she had previously denied was even needed, and ultimately to receive God's healing.

Living in denial is living a lie. It means we refuse to be swayed by the facts, no matter how they add up. We say to ourselves, "If I pretend this isn't happening, it will go away" or "If I tell myself this is something else, it *will* be." This self-protective measure kicks in when things appear to be completely out of our control. We block the situation from our mind or deny its existence in order to survive.

God's Spirit of truth is necessary to penetrate the darkness of self-deception. Merely confronting someone who is living in denial doesn't often work. To rip away this form of survival is to rip flesh from bone. The pain is unbearable. It's not simply a matter of peeling away dead skin; this false skin is deeply attached and grown together with the real flesh. There has to be healing from within so that what has been attached from the outside will fall away. Any confrontation with someone in deep denial must be preceded by much prayer and completely *led* by the Holy Spirit.

Facing the Truth

Many people don't want to spend any time at all dealing with the past. They often cite the passage in Scripture where the apostle Paul says we should be "forgetting those things which are behind and reaching forward to those things which are ahead" (Phil. 3:13). But what he means is that we shouldn't be living in the past from which we've been set *free*. Yet we can't be set free from something we have not brought into the full light of God and exposed for what it is. Only when we do that will we find healing for it, and only then can we forget and move on.

If you live in denial about anything, you will keep coming around to the same problem over and over again. "Why doesn't this situation ever change? Why can't I ever get beyond it?" you'll ask. And the answer will be that the Spirit of truth has not been allowed to shine His light upon it.

We have to look at our lives and ask ourselves the following questions. As you work through this introspection, ask God to reveal any place in your life where you are denying the truth. Then shine the truth of God's Word upon that situation. The Psalms tell us, "The LORD is gracious and full of compassion, slow to anger and great in mercy. The LORD is good to all" (145:8–9).

Think about how you feel:

1. The last time I felt unhappy, the following things were happening (for instance, my husband was gone on a business trip):

2. The time before that, the following things were happening (my closest friends went away for the weekend and didn't include me):

3. When I was a child, I was unhappy when (my dad was away for long periods of time):

4. Is there anything similar about the events in all of these situations? (I tend to feel lonely and abandoned when my husband is gone or my friends are gone because my father was gone so often.)

5. I may be unhappy because (I feel abandoned):

Think about your relationships:

1. The last time I disagreed with my spouse or a friend was because (for instance, they questioned my judgment about something as if I couldn't make a sound decision):

2. I feel unhappy with my boss at work when (he wants to know every detail of what I'm doing, as if he's checking up on me):

3. As a child I became angry with my parents when (they quizzed me incessantly about where I'd been and what I was doing):

4. Some of my anger at my spouse or my friend or my boss might relate back to (my dad's efforts to control everything I did):

Think about your relationship with God:

1. I think of God as (for instance, as a firm disciplinarian who expects me to be perfect):

2. I think of my father or my mother as (distant and always expecting too much of me):

3. My relationship with my father (or mother) might be influencing my relationship with God in the following ways:

Seeing the truth about yourself, your life, and your past is crucial to your healing. The longer you go on denying a problem, the longer it will take you to find wholeness. Had my father faced the problem of my mother head-on, a good psychiatrist might have helped her overcome her illness through counseling and medication. All those years of misery and destruction might never have happened.

Make No Room for Denial

God is the only one who can keep us out of denial. That's why we have to frequently pray, "Lord keep me undeceived and help me never to deny Your truth. If there is any place in my life where I have been deceiving myself, shine the light of Your Word upon it and bring Your Spirit of truth to rule there. Show me where I have rationalized anything that I should have faced. Where have I swept something under the rug that should have been thrown out? Where have I justified myself when I should have simply confessed? Please show me everything because I truly want to know."

Remember, sin is missing the mark. If we think we are without error all the time, whom are we kidding? I know someone who, when several friends confronted her about possible denial in her life, went to other friends who did not know the situation as well and built a case for what she wanted to believe instead of going to God and praying, "Show me the truth, Lord. If what these people are saying is right, help me to see it. If it isn't right, help *them* to see that too." As long as we depend on lies to insulate us from pain, we don't need to depend on God, and this will always keep us from experiencing all He has for us.

We are *all* victims of self-deception at one time or another. We do it expertly. That's why we can never be critical of another who lives in denial. We can only recognize it and pray for that person's eyes to be opened. But we are just as able to fall prey to self-deception if we are not seeking to

What the Bible Says About Denial

You desire truth in the inward parts,
And in the hidden part You will make me
to know wisdom.
—*Psalm 51:6*

I have no greater joy than to hear that my
children walk in truth.
—*3 John 4*

You shall know the truth, and the truth
shall make you free.
—*John 8:32*

For the wrath of God is revealed from
heaven against all ungodliness and
unrighteousness of men, who suppress
the truth in unrighteousness.
—*Romans 1:18*

When He, the Spirit of truth, has come,
He will guide you into all truth.
—*John 16:13*

have God's light shine on our lives. Pray frequently for the power of God to penetrate any form of denial in you.

Reject the Pitfall of Depression

The lie we believe when we feel depressed is *I cannot live with my situation the way it is, and I am powerless to change it.* When the discouragement of that belief settles over us like a thick fog, we can't see any way out of the darkness. The deception is in thinking that our situation is hopeless. This thought can be so subtle that we don't even realize it until we fall into a full-fledged depression.

Check any statements below that express feelings you've had in the last year:

○ I am weary with my groaning; all night I make my bed swim; I drench my couch with my tears. My eye wastes away because of grief; it grows old because of all my enemies. (Ps. 6:6–7)

○ [I *was*] troubled on every side. Outside were conflicts, inside were fears. (2 Cor. 7:5)

○ My soul is exceedingly sorrowful, even to death. (Matt. 26:38)

○ How long shall I take counsel in my soul, having sorrow in my heart daily? (Ps. 13:2)

○ The enemy has persecuted my soul; He has crushed my life to the ground; He has made me dwell in darkness, like those who have long been dead. (Ps. 143:3)

○ My spirit is overwhelmed within me, my heart within me is distressed. (Ps. 143:4)

If you checked any of these statements, you have definitely suffered depression. Sleepless nights, lying awake with your heart pounding. Feeling weak and crushed as if you're sinking into a deep, dark pit. When you look at yourself in the mirror the next morning, there is no light in your face, and your eyes are dull. You can tell people don't want to be around you. You feel like you can't emotionally connect with anyone. If you've ever been depressed, you know those feelings. So have many people who love God. Most of these Bible quotations were written by two great men who were dear to God's heart: David, the giant killer and king, and the apostle Paul. Both found God to be the ultimate answer to their depression. Obviously, depression is not unknown to the Lord.

One of the biggest deceptions about depression is thinking you are the only one who has ever felt depressed. Millions of people are depressed right now and feel exactly the way these people felt thousands of years ago. That fact may not reduce your depression, but at least you know you are not alone.

Some common symptoms of depression are troubled sleep, sleeping too much, constant fatigue, weight loss, excessive weight gain due to compulsive eating, poor concentration and memory, a high degree of self-criticism, extreme difficulty in making even the simplest decisions, suicidal thoughts, an inclination toward isolation, a negative outlook, feelings of failure, an inability to finish anything, a sense of being overwhelmed by even the slightest pressure, being gripped with sadness and discouragement, or an inability to handle the most menial of tasks.

Some of us live with these kinds of feelings so much we begin to accept them as a part of life. But they are not. Depression is not God's will for our lives. I battled depression until I was in my early thirties. Feeling utterly hopeless about anything ever being any different in my life had led me to the point of suicide. After I came to the Lord, my first major deliverance was from depression. The enormous amounts of unconfessed sin in my life had separated me from God's presence and power. Now when I'm threatened by depression, I recognize that something is out of order in my life or my mind, and I take it immediately to the Lord.

Taking Action Against It

Unless you take definite steps to stop depression, it snowballs. You feel worse and worse about yourself, others, and God, which further distances and depresses you.

If you struggle with occasional bouts of depression, or are depressed right now, I suggest that you go before the Lord and ask the same questions I ask:

1. *Is there any physical problem that could be causing this?* Depression can be caused by any number of physical situations such as hormone changes, menstrual periods, PMS, menopause, lack of sleep, drugs, alcohol, certain medications, overexertion, disease, lack of exercise, fatigue, allergies, and poor eating habits. Ask God to show you if anything physical is causing or contributing to your depression.

2. *Is there anyone or any circumstance that is causing this depression?* There may be a tangible reason for your depression. For example, having someone living in your house who is extremely negative and depressed can affect you. If you can think of anything like that, ask God what you can do to alter the situation. Can you speak to the person or do something to change things? Is there some possibility you're not seeing or never imagined? Sometimes depression signals that a major

change is needed. Ask God to show you the burdens you shouldn't be carrying and the changes that need to be made.

3. *Is there any sin I haven't confessed?* Sometimes the cause of depression is external (being exposed to something ungodly). Sometimes it is an attack by the devil (especially when God is doing a powerful work in your life). But most of the time it is caused by wrong thinking or action (an inappropriate response to a person or situation). Any negative feelings or bad attitudes need to be confessed—*especially unforgiveness.* You are the one who will suffer depression because of them, so ask God to show you any area where repentance is needed.

4. *Have I prayed about my depression?* One of the biggest traps or deceptions of depression is thinking you have no control over it. Too often we don't pray because we accept the depression as being a part of life instead of recognizing it as an emotional sickness like a cold or the flu, which needs attention before it turns into a more serious infection. You need to tell God exactly how you feel and ask Him to take your depression.

Remember that *God is on your side and the devil is your enemy.* Pastor Jack taught me, "You have to wait at Jesus' feet through the darkness. There is no night so long or so dark but that if you stay at the feet of the Lord, He will take care of it in the morning." Psalm 30:5 says, "Weeping may endure for a night, but joy comes in the morning."

If you wake up in the night with your heart pounding in fear or depression, get up immediately and go to your prayer closet and pray and read the Word. Go back to sleep when you can, and then continue praying the next day. Often when people

What the Bible Says About Depression

Then they cried out to the LORD in their
trouble, and He saved them out of their dis-
tresses. He brought them out of
darkness and the shadow of death,
And broke their chains in pieces.
—*Psalm 107:13–14*

If I say, "My foot slips,"
Your mercy, O LORD, will hold me up.
In the multitude of my anxieties within me
Your comforts delight my soul.
—*Psalm 94:18–19*

The righteous cry out and the LORD hears
them; he delivers them from all their troubles.
The LORD is close to the brokenhearted and
saves those who are crushed in spirit.
—*Psalm 34:17–18 NIV*

Those who hope in the LORD will renew
their strength. They will soar on wings like
eagles; they will run and not grow weary,
they will walk and not be faint.
—*Isaiah 40:31*

don't get an immediate answer to their prayers, they stop turning to God and try to work it out on their own. Don't do that.

5. *What lies am I listening to?* If you are depressed, you probably have accepted a lie as the truth—usually a lie about yourself: "You're a failure. You're no good. You won't make it. You're ugly." But all of this is in direct opposition to Scripture, which says you have special gifts and talents. The fact that the world isn't recognizing your gifts at this moment doesn't mean they aren't there or that you are worthless. Dispel lies with the truth of God's Word.

6. *Which of God's promises can I quote aloud to sum up His perspective as it relates to me or my situation?* God's Word says, "Anxiety in the heart of man causes depression, but a good word makes it glad" (Prov. 12:25). This good word could come from a pastor, a friend, a spouse, a family member, or a nice person on the street, but we can't depend on human beings. The good word that will truly make your heart glad will come from the Lord through *His* Word. There are an abundance of them, but I have listed just a few in this chapter. When you find a promise or word from Him that speaks to your situation, underline it or write it on paper and tape it to your bathroom mirror. Speak it aloud whenever you feel depressed. Even when you feel nothing is happening, continue speaking God's Word aloud; eventually your spirit and soul will respond to the hope and truth.

It's also good to adapt a Scripture to your situation by speaking it aloud, like this:

"When *I* pass through the waters, *You* will be with *me;* when
I pass through the waters, they shall not overflow *me.* When

I walk through the fire, I shall not be burned, nor shall the flame scorch *me*." (Isa. 43:2). [Italics added to show how to personalize a Scripture.]

7. *How much have I praised, worshiped, and thanked God in the midst of my depression?* Being depressed is a sign that your personality has turned inward and focused on itself. One of the healthiest steps to take is to focus outwardly on God through praise. Stop everything you're doing and say: "Lord, I praise You. I worship You. I give thanks to You. I glorify You. I love You. I exalt Your name. I refuse to give depression a hold in my life, and I praise You, Lord, that Your joy is my strength." Thanking Him for everything you can think of is the best way to stop the stream of self-abuse that goes through your head.

I've also found that clapping my hands and singing praise to the Lord is unbeatable for bringing relief from a spirit of heaviness. This is the last thing you feel like doing when you're depressed, but you have to decide that you *don't* want depression and you *do* want all that God has for you. Don't give up until you've won this battle.

When Nothing Helps

If you've asked yourself these questions and done all that's been suggested and are still deeply depressed, then you need to seek out a Christian counselor. If you can't get a counseling appointment until a week from Tuesday, make yourself get up each day and do at least two things. You could wash the dishes, make the bed, pull some weeds in the yard, sweep the garage, put one load of clothes in the washing machine, wash your car, or clean out a drawer. Whatever it is, do it and don't worry about anything else at this moment. Then take your Bible, sit down with the Lord, and take comfort in the fact that your life has some order and you have accomplished something.

And don't let not-so-well-meaning, self-righteous people convince you that if you were really born again, you wouldn't be depressed. Suggest that they tell that to King David and the apostle Paul!

Because of Jesus, you *can* win over depression.

Reject the Pitfall of Envy

Years ago, I walked into a friend's house and was struck by how much I enjoyed the spaciousness and the light, airy feel of the home. I thought, *That's what I would like someday.* I did not want *her* house. I did not feel sad or resentful that *she* had the house. I didn't go home and hate *my* house. I didn't say, "I must have a house like that immediately!" But I did think, *I like that quality in a house, and if I'm ever given a choice, I would choose that.* Ten years later when Michael and I were looking for another home to move into, we chose one with many skylights and windows, which created that same feeling of spaciousness. I acknowledged the good that someone else had, but I did not envy.

I aspire to be as good a writer as some of my favorite authors. But I do not want to be given credit for writing their books. Nor do I long for people to say I'm better than they are. I certainly don't want to copy their style. And I don't desire that they fail. I just want to be able to touch people with that same depth and impact as they do. I admire, but I do not envy.

If I felt miserable every time I walked into another person's house that was better than mine or if I felt bad every time I read a great new book, then I would be envious. Envy destroys the soul.

The lie we believe when we are envious of someone is "I need and deserve to have what he has." The truth is that everything we have comes from God. To have sorrow, discontent, or ill will over someone else's possessions or advantages is to reject what God *has* given us and what He is *able* to give to us. The deception of envy is thinking that God doesn't have enough to go around. What someone else has then becomes a threat to our well-being.

The New Bible Dictionary describes *covetousness* as "selfish desire" and "in essence the worship of self." It is the ultimate idolatry, and *idolatry is the root of envy.* The Bible says we are to put to death "covetousness, which is idolatry" (Col. 3:5) because it will undermine the purposes of God in our lives. The writer of Proverbs also makes this very clear: "A sound heart is life to the body, but envy is rottenness to the bones" (Prov. 14:30).

Covetousness destroys the very core of our being and causes our inner strength to crumble. If unforgiveness is the cancer of the soul, then envy is the osteoporosis!

The Fine Line Between Envy and Admiration

Envy was not part of my early life because I believed I didn't deserve anything anyway. I always wanted more than I had because I had nothing, and I felt sorry for myself when I didn't get it. But I didn't begrudge others for having it. However, I coveted other people's abilities to speak or sing. My own vocal problems from early childhood on never improved as much as I wanted them to, and I felt cheated.

One day as I read the Bible, the Lord spoke to my heart through a verse that says, "Where envy and self-seeking exist, confusion and every evil thing are there" (James 3:16). It was as if the Lord pointed to my heart and said, "You have confusion in your life right now because of the envy and self-seeking in your heart."

How embarrassed I felt. *Me? Have envy?* But I knew that constantly measuring myself against others was the seed from which envy grows. I couldn't live in peace if I hung on to it.

To be free I had to do four things:

- I had to take stock of all that God had given me and be thankful for it.

- I had to come to terms with my limitations and strictly avoid comparing myself with others.

- I had to make myself be thankful to God for other people's talents, gifts, and abilities.

- I had to remind myself of what *my* calling was from God and not demand to have someone else's.

It was a matter of being able to say, "Lord, You created me and You know what will fulfill me. Forgive me for coveting the gifts of other people. Release me from the bondage of envy, and set me free from the agony of desiring anything that is not mine to have. I realize that what You have for me is better than anything I could covet for myself."

To decide whether what you feel is envy or admiration, you need to assess your motives honestly. Check the following statements that apply to your present attitudes:

○ I constantly compare myself with others.

○ I secretly feel good when someone fails or has something bad happen to him.

○ When I see how good someone is at what she does, rather than appreciate it I immediately berate myself for not being as good.

○ I don't like to be around certain people because their talents, appearance, or possessions make me feel inferior.

○ I feel bad when my friends or neighbors get something new (car, clothes, furniture).

○ When I see someone get something new, I feel I must have the same thing.

○ When I see bad qualities in a certain person, I want others to see them too.

○ I don't like to visit people who live in a nicer house because it makes me feel as if my house is not as good.

If you've checked any of the above, envy is trying to get hold of your heart. Call a halt to it, repent, and let it go.

Envy will put great limitations on your life. If you are envious of what someone has, you will either never have that yourself, or you will get it and won't be satisfied by it. The Bible asks, "Who is able to stand before jealousy?" (Prov. 27:4). Who, indeed, can live with it and not feel its crushing weight? Whether *in* you or directed *at* you, envy is evil. Satan fell from heaven because he wanted what God had. It will be your downfall, too, if you entertain it, and you will never become the whole person God created you to be. Find the peace of knowing that everything you have is from the Lord.

What the Bible Says About Envy

God gave them over to a debased mind, to
do those things which are not fitting; being
filled with all unrighteousness, sexual
immorality, wickedness, covetousness,
maliciousness; full of envy, murder, strife,
deceit, evil-mindedness . . . that those who
practice such things are deserving of death.

—Romans 1:28–29, 32

For we ourselves were also once foolish,
disobedient, deceived, serving various lusts
and pleasures, living in malice and envy,
hateful and hating one another.

—Titus 3:3

For where there are envy, strife, and
divisions among you, are you not carnal
and behaving like mere men?

—1 Corinthians 3:3

Love does not envy.

—1 Corinthians 13:4

You shall not covet your neighbor's
house . . . nor anything that is
your neighbor's.

—Exodus 20:17

Reject the Pitfall of Fear

Fear was the controlling factor of my life before I received Jesus: fear of failure, of bodily harm, of being emotionally hurt, of getting old, of being a nobody. An aching, paralyzing, all-engulfing spirit of fear had overtaken me, bringing with it companion spirits of suicide, despair, anxiety, and hopelessness. As I fought to keep from drowning in my fears, I ran out of strength. Gradually my fear of life overrode my fear of death, and suicide seemed as if it would be a pleasant relief.

I have heard it said many times that F-E-A-R stands for False Evidence Appearing Real. When the devil presents false evidence and makes it seem real, we can choose to listen to his falsehoods or believe God.

One of the biggest fears for anyone who has been emotionally damaged as a child is fear of the opinions of others. Our fears tell us, "People won't like me when they find out what I'm really like." But Isaiah 51:7 tells us, "Do not fear the reproach of men, nor be afraid of their insults." Because of Jesus, we *never* have to live in fear of the opinions of others.

Emotionally damaged people also often fear bodily harm. I used to be afraid to stay alone even in the daytime, and I could barely sleep at night because I feared that all the evil of the world would come upon me. I don't live with that kind of fear now that I've learned to live under God's protective covering.

The lie we believe when we are afraid is "God is not able to keep me and all that I care about safe." To be sure, there is much to be afraid of in this world, but when the strength of that fear outweighs our sense of God's presence, a spirit of fear can attach itself to our personality. If frightening or traumatizing things have happened to us in childhood, we believe this lie all the more. We think God is not in control of our situation.

The opposite of fear is faith, and we usually interpret the circumstances of our lives through one or the other. Fear causes us to live like we are emotionally paralyzed. We fear not having enough, so we don't give. We fear being hurt, so we hesitate to love. We fear being taken advantage of, so we don't serve others. We fear rejection, so we don't step out and do what God has called us to do.

What to Do When You Are Afraid

Realizing that fear doesn't come from God and you don't have to live in it is the first step in freeing yourself. Here are a few more things you can do when you are afraid:

1. *Confess your fear to the Lord and ask Him to free you from it.* Don't deny your fear. Take it to God instead and pray for deliverance. As you draw close to Him, His love will penetrate your life and crowd fear out.

If you are being controlled by strong fear, you are probably beset by a *spirit* of fear, which has to be cast out. In that case, say, "God, I confess my fear as sin before You and ask You to forgive me for it. Strengthen my faith in You and Your Word. I command you, spirit of fear, to be gone in the name of Jesus. Thank You, Lord, that You have not given me a spirit of fear, but of love, power, and a sound mind. Flood me with Your love and wash away all doubt."

2. *Check to see if there is, in fact, a very real danger, and do what you can to remedy the situation.* Have others pray with you until the danger passes and you have peace about it.

What the Bible Says About Fear

I sought the LORD, and He heard me,
And delivered me from all my fears.

—Psalm 34:4

Yea, though I walk through the valley of the
shadow of death, I will fear no evil: for thou
art with me; thy rod and thy staff, they
comfort me.

—Psalm 23:4

There is no fear in love; but perfect love
casts out fear, because fear involves torment. But he who fears has not been made
perfect in love.

—1 John 4:18

The LORD is my light and my salvation;
whom shall I fear? The LORD is the strength
of my life; of whom shall I be afraid?

—Psalm 27:1

Fear not, for I am with you; be not
dismayed, for I am your God.
I will strengthen you,
Yes, I will help you, I will uphold you with
My righteous right hand.

—Isaiah 41:10

3. *Commit to trust the Lord unquestioningly for seven days.* Decide that for one week you are going to believe that every promise in God's Word is completely true for you. Each day read the promises of God's protection in Psalm 91. Pick one verse to say aloud throughout the day and thank God for His promises to you in it. Each verse is full of God's love toward you. When you store them in your heart, they will crowd out fear.

4. *Worship the Lord out loud.* Praise is your greatest weapon against fear, so use it with great force. Clap your hands, sing, and speak praises to God. Thank Him for His great love. The more you do, the more you'll open up to receive it.

No matter what has happened to you or is happening in the world around you, God promises to protect you as you walk with Him. In fact, He is committed to protecting you all the time. We don't know how much evil the Lord protects us from every day, but I'm sure it's far more than we imagine. He is more powerful than any adversary we face, and He promises that no matter what the enemy brings into our lives, we will triumph in it.

The only fear you are to have is the fear of God, a respect for God's authority and power. Fearing God means fearing what life without Him would be and thanking Him continually that because of His love you'll never have to experience it.

Reject the Pitfall of Lust

The first lie we believe when we are tempted by lust is, *It doesn't hurt to think about it if I'm not actually going to do anything.* But every lustful act begins as a simple thought. We are deceived if we think we are too strong or too good to ever be tempted. Temptation will always present itself when our resistance is at its lowest and our soul is left unguarded.

Lust is an excessive desire to gratify *any* of the senses, but I am referring here to sexual desire, a specific spirit that comes to destroy your life by tempting you to think and do something you have already made a decision not to do.

I was attacked by such a spirit after I'd been married nearly five years and was about to enter a new phase in my ministry. I say attacked because it came out of nowhere—a sudden, overwhelming strong attraction to someone I had no interest in whatsoever. It was like being in an ocean wave that carried me away. I'm sure some people would interpret this attraction as fate or love or the perfect match. I already knew it was none of those because I was certain God had put my husband and me together, and I did not want to be with anyone else.

When this happened, I literally got on my face before the Lord, confessed those feelings, rebuked the spirit of lust, and cried out to God for deliverance. I struggled for several days, remaining in the Lord's presence (prayer, praise, the Word) while He fought the battle. When I woke up on the morning of the third day, it was *completely* gone. The war had ended, the Lord had won, and I had been liberated. If it had gone on any longer, I would have gone to a Christian counselor for prayer. But I knew the victory was complete, for whenever I saw that person again there was absolutely no attraction. In fact, I thought, *How could I have even been tempted?*

Trust the Lord, Not Your Heart

The Bible says, "He who trusts in his own heart is a fool, but whoever walks wisely will be delivered" (Prov. 28:26).

I would have been a fool to have trusted in my own heart.

I could have lost everything. I now believe the devil came to tempt me and the Lord allowed me to be proved, as He did Job. I'm convinced that the decision I made determined the course of my life and the release of my ministry.

I know from experience that a spirit of lust is powerful. People who are weak in the Lord don't have the strength to resist it. But if we handle it properly, the temptation will expose any weaknesses in ourselves and the marriage. I realized, for example, that my husband and I had become too busy to nurture ourselves as a couple. Michael's work was thriving, he was gone a lot and inattentive to my needs, and I was insecure and vulnerable. The atmosphere was ripe for the devil to move in.

Married people fall into adultery, and single people fall into sexual failure because a spirit of lust tempts them with lies like:

- "No one will know."
  The truth is, God knows.

- "I can handle this."
  The truth is that the spirit of lust is too strong for human flesh to resist.

- "This is all in fun; it's nothing serious."
  The truth is, Satan is behind a spirit of lust, and he is always serious about your destruction.

- "I know what I'm doing."
  The truth is, anyone under the influence of lust is being deceived, so you can't possibly know what you are doing.

Watch out for these thoughts. Take an attitude check every once in a while so you can beware of this spirit. If you are married, check these *Danger Signs for a Married Person:*

○ I have even the slightest hint of a sexual or emotional attraction to someone other than my spouse.

○ I can't get that person out of my mind, and I daydream about what it would be like to be with that person in different settings (in a restaurant, walking together, etc.).

○ I make decisions or dress with that person in mind.

○ I feel self-conscious when I'm in this person's presence.

○ I go out of my way to be with this person.

○ I imagine what that person might think of the way I look or what I'm doing.

○ I am extra nice to my husband (wife) so he (she) won't notice how attentive I am to the other person.

○ I imagine what it would be like to be married to that person.

○ I feel guilty about the thoughts I have toward this person.

If you are single, check these *Danger Signs for a Single Person:*

○ I am obsessed with sexual thoughts about a certain person.

○ I feel a sexual drive toward this person that I fear I will be unable to control.

○ I think of this person as a sexual object more than as a brother (or sister) in the Lord.

○ My primary goal for this person is to meet my needs, rather than helping him (her) become what God made him (her) to be.

○ I am unable to confess my deepest feelings about this person to the Lord.

○ When I come before the Lord, my thoughts about this person don't make me feel clean.

○ I look for Bible verses that might justify my feelings about him (her).

○ I doubt the validity of Scripture if it suggests that I restrict my relationship with him (her).

○ I allow myself to venture into dangerous territory by being alone with this person when I know I shouldn't.

If you come in contact with someone for whom you feel a strong sexual attraction, immediately rebuke the devil. Say, "I bind you, Satan, and refuse to let you destroy my life with temptation. Sexual immorality is a sin against God, and I don't want any part of it. By the power of the Holy Spirit, I smash any hold the spirit of lust has on my life."

Then go before the Lord in prayer. And I mean lie down in your prayer closet on your face and cry out to God. Say, "Lord, I confess my attraction to this person and these sexual thoughts that come to my mind. Forgive me and set me free from them. Show me, God, why Satan thinks he can attack me in this area. Help me not to be deceived but to see everything clearly. I praise You, Lord, that You are more powerful than any temptation I face." Stay there before the Lord, praising Him for His grace, love, and goodness until you feel the pressure lifted.

If you leave the safety of the Lord's presence before the battle is under control, you can step into dangerous territory and get shot down, seriously maimed, or even mortally wounded.

Don't play around with this kind of fire. It's attached to an explosive with the power to do irreparable damage.

After the Fall

If you've already fallen into the devil's trap and acted on a spirit of lust, you need to receive deliverance. Don't try to handle it on your own. Get help. Go to a counselor, a Christian therapist, a pastor, church elders, a prayer group, or a strong believer who will keep your confidence. Have that person pray for you to be free. If you don't, you won't be. After deliverance, expect an extended time of healing. Find help for that too.

Every time you feel tempted by this spirit again, confess it to whomever you have chosen to help you. Absolutely do *not* be alone with the person you are attracted to. It's best not to see him (her) at all, but if it cannot be avoided, be sure at least one other person is with you at all times.

As Christians, we are to forsake even the appearance of evil, and so it is with lust. We know when we have crossed from mere observation into the realm of attraction or desire. At that time, even a meeting of the eyes can be a manifestation of evil. You have to decide *now* that you will resist lust in every way until it no longer makes any appearance at all.

Check to see if any temptation in your life is encouraged by problems in your marriage, bondage in your life, or wounds from the past. Or is your ministry about to advance and destroy some of the devil's territory? If it is, he will be right there with a spirit of lust (either sexual or a quest for power or both) to try to stop you. Take it seriously. We have seen him succeed far too often. Lust is a pit waiting for all of us. Decide now that you will not allow Satan the satisfaction of seeing you fall into it.

What the Bible Says About Lust

For this is the will of God, your sanctification: that
you should abstain from sexual immorality; that
each of you should know how to possess his own
vessel in sanctification and honor, not in passion
of lust, like the Gentiles who do not know God.

—1 Thessalonians 4:3–5

No temptation has overtaken you except such as
is common to man; but God is faithful, who will
not allow you to be tempted beyond what you are
able, but with the temptation will also make the
way of escape, that you may be able to bear it.

—1 Corinthians 10:13

Abstain from fleshly lusts which
war against the soul.

—1 Peter 2:11

The righteousness of the upright will
deliver them, but the unfaithful will be
caught by their lust.

—Proverbs 11:6

Blessed is the man who endures temptation;
for when he has been approved, he will
receive the crown of life which the Lord has
promised to those who love Him.

—James 1:12

Reject the Pitfall of Lying

Most people don't realize how lying damages the soul. It separates us from God. And we can't have wholeness without the Lord's presence. God can't bring you into close communion with Himself until His truth controls your heart.

The deception of lying is thinking that a lie will make things better for you. Actually, it does the opposite. Telling a lie means that you have aligned yourself with the spirit of lies, which is Satan. *Lying means you have just given the devil a piece of your heart.* Allowing Satan to have any part of you opens you to his kingdom. The more you lie, the greater his hold on you, and once you are bound by a lying spirit, you won't be able to stop yourself from lying.

I learned to lie as a child because I felt that the consequences of telling the truth were too great. Also I was so embarrassed about my life that lying to others was far more tolerable than admitting the truth. One of the lies I frequently told was about my age. In our small town in Wyoming, the one school was so crowded that unless you were six years old by the time school started on September 14, you had to wait until the following year to start first grade. (There was no kindergarten.) My birthday was on September 16, so I had to wait and start the next year. When we moved to California during the summer before I started fourth grade, I turned ten the day before school started. Everyone else in the class was nine. When the other children found out, I was teased mercilessly about having flunked a grade.

The next time we moved to a different city, I decided to lie about my age. I continued that lie through high school, college, and the years I worked as an actress, singer, and dancer on television. The entertainment business was so youth-oriented that I sometimes lopped off as much as five years from my age. I lived in terror that someone would find out. Once, when someone did, I was mortified.

When I came to know the Lord and started living His way, I realized I couldn't align myself with the author of lies and the Spirit of truth at the same time. I decided that I wanted people to know everything about me so they could accept or reject me on the basis of who I really am. It was a big relief to be freed from the fear of people finding out I was lying to them, and as far as I know, no one has ever rejected me because of my age. It's amazing how your feelings of self-worth rise sharply when you know you are living in truth.

Lying As a Means of Survival

People who have been physically or emotionally abused learn to lie to protect themselves or to make themselves feel better. Even though such lying is thoroughly understandable, it's still lying and can lead to emotional imbalance and even mental illness. Lies start becoming so real to the person telling them that they begin to believe them themselves.

This is what happened to my mother. When she was eleven, her mother died suddenly and tragically. Because her father was unable to care for her and her two sisters, they were sent to various homes to live. When my mother finally became attached to another family, the father in that family committed suicide. The deaths of her mother and then this foster parent several years later were so traumatic that she never recovered.

She told me many times that she was responsible for both deaths. She'd had an argument with her mother the night she went into the hospital and died, and my mother's guilt and remorse lasted for the rest of her life. She also believed her foster father killed himself because she came to live with them during the Great Depression and was an added burden. My mother's self-imposed guilt over all this was too unbearable for her to handle, so she created a world all her own that she *could* handle. In her world, lies became her reality and she never had to face the truth. If she'd had good Christian therapy, or at least a family who prayed her through this time of trauma, she might have been spared her tragic life of mental torture. She was an extreme example of the result of a lying spirit.

The Bible says, "Getting treasures by a lying tongue is the fleeting fantasy of those who seek death" (Prov. 21:6). How could it be said more clearly? The consequences of telling the truth have to be better than death.

If you are aware of falling into the pit of lying, you must confess every lie to God immediately. The moment you find you have lied, say, "Lord, I confess before You that I have lied, and as a result, have aligned myself with Satan. God, forgive me for that and cleanse me of all evil. Satan, I refuse to be a part of your deception and evil, and I command your lying spirit to be gone in the name of Jesus. I praise You, Lord, that You are the God of truth and have the power to make all things new."

Next, immerse yourself in God's truth, His Word. Ask the Spirit of truth—the Holy Spirit—to flow through you and cleanse you from all lies. Ask God to show you any other lie that you are speaking or living. Lying keeps you from enjoying healthy relationships (Prov. 26:28), and it separates you from the presence of the Lord: "He who tells lies shalt not continue in my presence" (Ps. 101:7). You can't have emotional health and happiness without the presence of God in your life.

Remember every lie from your lips means you have given a piece of your heart to the devil, who fills that hole with confusion, emotional and mental illness, and death. Don't allow him the pleasure. Instead, choose the way of truth.

What the Bible Says About Lying

Let not mercy and truth forsake you;
Bind them around your neck,
Write them on the tablet of your heart,
And so find favor and high esteem
In the sight of God and man.

—Proverbs 3:3–4

Lying lips are an abomination to the LORD,
But those who deal truthfully
are His delight.

—Proverbs 12:22

Deliver my soul, O LORD, from lying lips
And from a deceitful tongue.

—Psalm 120:2

A lying tongue hates those who
are crushed by it.

—Proverbs 26:28

My soul melts from heaviness;
Strengthen me according to Your word.
Remove from me the way of lying.

—Psalm 119:28–29

Reject the Pitfall of Perfectionism

It's miserable to try to be perfect all the time. And it's exhausting as well. We try to be perfect in order to be acceptable to ourselves and to others, but in reality, the more perfect we try to make ourselves, the more uncomfortable we make the people around us. People aren't looking for someone to be perfect for them; they're looking for someone to love them. The deception of perfectionism is in thinking that anyone other than God can ever be perfect.

For years I wouldn't write anything for people to see because I knew what I wrote wasn't perfect. I also wouldn't invite people to my house for dinner because my house and my cooking weren't perfect. I wouldn't see people when I didn't look perfect, and I wouldn't talk to them on the phone when I wasn't feeling perfect. Living every day with the pressure to be perfect nearly suffocated me.

Perfect in Love

I once wrote a magazine article in which I said, "God never asks us to be perfect; He simply asks us to take steps of obedience." Someone wrote to me afterward, saying, "How can you say that when Matthew 5:48 clearly says, 'You shall be perfect, just as your Father in heaven is perfect.' "

In a responding article, I wrote that the definition of *perfect* in the *New World Dictionary* is "complete in all respects, flawless, faultless, without defect, in a condition of complete excellence." If we use this definition, Jesus is saying, "You must be faultless, without defect, and completely excellent! Now!" That's impossible!

People who feel God expects this level of performance put pressure on themselves to attain it. Then they feel like failures when they fall short. But the good news is that the Word of God doesn't say that at all.

So what did Jesus mean when He said, "Be perfect, therefore, as your heavenly Father is perfect" (Matt. 5:48 NIV)? It's explained a few verses earlier, where Jesus said, "You have heard that it was said, 'You shall love your neighbor and hate your enemy.' But I say to you, love your enemies, bless those who curse you, do good to those who hate you, and pray for those who spitefully use you and persecute you" (Matt. 5:43–44). The passage goes on to say that if you love as God loves, you shall be perfect, just as your Father in heaven is perfect. In other words, if we are motivated in all we do by love for God, which overflows into love for others, we shall be perfected. *Being perfect has to do with the condition of the heart.*

One day my six-year-old, Amanda, picked roses for me from our backyard because she knew how much I love flowers. While she was getting my favorite vase down from the shelf, she dropped it on the tile floor, and it smashed into a hundred pieces. She was devastated and so was I, but I didn't punish her because I recognized that her *heart* was perfect, even though her *performance* was not. She was doing what she did out of love, even though she was not able to accomplish it perfectly. The perfection God expects from us is just like that.

A heart that is pure in love toward God is a heart that desires to obey Him. God knows our actions can never be 100 percent perfect. That's why He sent Jesus. Through Him, God has given us access to the perfection only God can provide. Our hearts can be perfect even if our actions are not.

We who were abused as children are already painfully aware of our imperfections. We need to know that God

What the Bible Says About Perfectionism

But this Man, after He had offered one sacrifice for sins forever, sat down at the right hand of God, from that time waiting till His enemies are made His footstool. For by one offering He has perfected forever those who are being sanctified.

—Hebrews 10:12–14

Him we preach, warning every man and teaching every man in all wisdom, that we may present every man perfect in Christ Jesus.

—Colossians 1:28

Not that I have already attained, or am already perfected; but I press on, that I may lay hold of that for which Christ Jesus has also laid hold of me.

—Philippians 3:12

But may the God of all grace, who called us to His eternal glory by Christ Jesus, after you have suffered a while, perfect, establish, strengthen, and settle you.

—1 Peter 5:10

It is God who arms me with strength,
And makes my way perfect.

—Psalm 18:32

doesn't expect us to be perfect in *performance* but perfect in *heart*. We need to know that God *already* views us as perfect when He looks into our hearts and sees Jesus there. Failure to understand this can keep us forever striving for the unattainable and eventually giving up because we feel we can never be all we "should" be.

God says He wants to make you something *more* than your human excellence can ever be. He wants to love you into wholeness. You will rise to the level and degree that you sense His love in your life. That's why I can now invite people to my home, cook for them, speak to them, and write to them. I don't have to worry about being perfect because the perfection of Christ is manifested by His love flowing through me.

When you look in the mirror and see the excellence of Jesus reflected back, that's when you will have a sense of your true worth. The actual transformation takes place every time you worship the Lord for *His* perfection.

Reject the Pitfall of Pride

Oddly enough, pride is one of the biggest problems for someone who has been emotionally damaged. It's hard to spot because it is so hidden inside and covered with feelings of low self-worth. I always believed I didn't have pride. In fact, I took pride in that. But it wasn't true. When I was working as a television entertainer, I feared failure even more than I desired success. This fear of failure was not humility, but pride. I felt I deserved to be successful. But my pride made me all the more susceptible to failure.

The lie we believe when we are prideful is *I'm in control of my life, I'm important, and I can make things happen the way*

I want them to happen. The opposite—humility—says, "Without God I am nothing, but I can do all things through Christ who strengthens me."

The deception of pride is thinking that our will is more important than God's will. This was Satan's downfall. He didn't want to let God be God and do things God's way. His last words before he was cast out of heaven were "I will exalt my throne above the stars of God" (Isa. 14:13). He was perfect before pride took root in his heart and he decided God's will was no longer as important as his own. But "God resists the proud" and "gives grace to the humble" (James 4:6). Without God's grace we fall.

A Mask for Fear

Pride comes from being afraid that you have no value as a person. It says, "I have to be great because I fear I'll be nothing." At the opposite extreme is the thought, *If I can't be the best, then I'll be the worst. If I can't make people love me, then I'll make them hate me.* Prisons are crowded with people who have felt that way.

The more spiritually mature we become, the more we see that without God we are nothing. It is *He* who gives us our worth: "For if anyone thinks himself to be something, when he is nothing, he deceives himself" (Gal. 6:3). The writer of Proverbs advises us, "Do not be wise in your own eyes; fear the LORD and depart from evil. It will be health to your flesh, and strength to your bones" (3:7–8).

It takes a lot of healing to come from feeling like a nothing to accepting your worth in Jesus, then to admitting that apart from God you are nothing. But when you can do that, it will be God *in* you that leads you to greatness. Ask God to give you a humble heart. He will.

What the Bible Says About Pride

Pride goes before destruction,
And a haughty spirit before a fall.
—*Proverbs 16:18*

They have humbled themselves; therefore
I will not destroy them, but I will grant
them some deliverance.
—*2 Chronicles 12:7*

He who is of a proud heart stirs up strife,
But he who trusts in the LORD will
be prospered.
—*Proverbs 28:25*

A man's pride will bring him low,
But the humble in spirit will retain honor.
—*Proverbs 29:23*

Everyone proud in heart is an
abomination to the LORD.
—*Proverbs 16:5*

Reject the Pitfall of Rebellion

Without the Lord, we all walk in rebellion. But rebellion can happen in us even *after* we've received the Lord and are living in obedience. In fact, we can fall into rebellion without even realizing it.

One of the most common forms of rebellion among believers is spiritual apathy. We all know if we've just robbed a liquor store, murdered someone, or committed adultery. We're not as keen at recognizing when we have drifted away from the mainstream of God's Spirit in our lives.

A number of years ago, I had corrective surgery for an old childhood injury. The doctor's instructions were, "Stay home for two months and do no lifting, no bending, no walking, no exercising, no quick movements, and no straining." In other words, no life.

For the first couple of weeks, I was too groggy to read the Bible very much or do any in-depth praying, so I resorted to something I never do: I watched a lot of television and looked through many secular magazines. None of them were objectionable, but all the messages were from the world, telling me how to think, to look, to buy and sell, and to structure my home and marriage.

When my convalescence finally ended, I slowly made efforts to get back into my normal routine. But things were different. I didn't read the Bible as much, and I was too busy for the prayer closet, opting rather to pray and run. Soon I was running on my own steam instead of being sustained and guided by the Lord.

Slowly I began to make decisions for my life without asking God. I didn't think I was doing that, but the fruit of those decisions proved that I was. I began walking in rebellion by serving my own needs.

The lie we believe when we rebel against God is, *I think this is right for me, so I'm going to do it, no matter what God or anyone else says.* The deception of rebellion is in thinking that our way is better than God's. *Rebellion is pride put into action.*

The Bible says, "Rebellion is as the sin of witchcraft" (1 Sam. 15:23). Witchcraft is, of course, total opposition to God. The same verse says that stubbornness is idolatry. Pride *puts* us in rebellion. Stubbornness *keeps* us in rebellion. *There is an idol in the life of anyone who walks stubbornly in rebellion. Identifying and smashing that idol is the key to coming back into alignment with God.* We want what we want. See what it is that you want. If it doesn't line up with God's will, it's an idol.

Spiritual Apathy

The danger once we know the Lord and have been walking His way is thinking that we have learned the lessons. We've read the Bible. We're receiving the blessings. And now we believe we can let things slide. We become lazy in what we have already learned to do. We let church attendance become a lower priority, allow our giving to slack off, and look the other way when certain steps of obedience fall by the wayside—while the enemy sneaks up on our blind side.

Too many battles have been lost by just this sort of rebellion. Only we don't call it rebellion—not we seasoned Christians—we call it "maturity." *After* the fact, we call it "stupidity." Because all of us are susceptible to spiritual apathy, "we must give the more earnest heed to the things we have heard, lest we drift away" (Heb. 2:1).

Do you wonder if you are falling into rebellion by drifting spiritually? A number of warning signs can help you prevent such a fall. Periodically check the following statements that apply to you:

○ I am allowing outer sources like TV, magazines, movies, and books to mold me more than the Holy Spirit does.

○ I'm influenced more by what my friends say than by what the Lord is telling me.

○ I am becoming spiritually malnourished because I am not *daily* feeding on the Word of God or feasting in His presence in prayer and praise.

○ I am beginning to think I've heard it all, so I have no reason to go to church or Bible study.

○ I've begun to do a few things I formerly avoided, ignoring what I've learned to be right, in favor of a new experience.

○ I've begun to make decisions without godly counsel because it *feels* right.

○ I haven't asked the Lord specifically about a major purchase, but it's something I've always wanted, so it must be God's will.

○ I haven't done anything wrong, so I don't need to ask God to reveal any unconfessed sin.

If you checked any item above, take it before the Lord in repentance immediately so that you can be taken off the path that leads to destruction.

Walking in the Will of God

The Bible says, "There is a way that seems right to a man, but its end is the way of death" (Prov. 16:25).

It can *seem* completely right when we are totally wrong.

What the Bible Says About Rebellion

If you are willing and obedient, you shall eat
the good of the land; but if you refuse and
rebel, you shall be devoured by the sword.

—Isaiah 1:19–20

Let them fall by their own counsels;
Cast them out in the multitude of their
transgressions, for they have
rebelled against You.

—Psalm 5:10

Those who sat in darkness and in the shadow
of death, bound in affliction and irons—
because they rebelled against the words of
God, and despised the counsel of the Most
High, therefore He brought down their
heart with labor; they fell down, and
there was none to help.

—Psalm 107:10–12

Nevertheless they were disobedient
and rebelled against You . . .
Therefore You delivered them into the hand
of their enemies, who oppressed them.

—Nehemiah 9:26–27

That's why we can't successfully determine the right path for ourselves. God alone knows it. We must look to Him to find the center of *His* will, for only there can we truly be safe. *Walking in His will is the opposite of walking in rebellion.*

When Michael and I were dating, I worried constantly that I might take matters concerning our relationship into my own hands and ruin everything. Over and over I prayed that God would keep me in His will about the relationship. I didn't want to make another mistake like I had with my short first marriage.

I did my best to keep from manipulating the outcome to what I thought would be my advantage. For example, when Michael didn't call me for a period of time, I resisted the temptation to contact him, no matter how lonely I felt. I didn't actively pursue him, even though my heart's desire was for this relationship to work out. When he finally did ask me to marry him, I was certain it was a prompting from the Lord and not the result of any sly maneuvers on my part.

The key to finding God's will, in this case, was to constantly give the situation entirely to the Lord, pray about it, praise Him for His perfect will in my life, and then wait on Him for the answer. Being in the center of God's will brings great security and confidence because there is something uniquely wonderful about knowing that you are exactly where you're supposed to be. It is a guaranteed place of safety and peace.

Walking in God's will also makes your life simpler. Oswald Chambers said, "If we have purpose of our own, it destroys the simplicity and the leisureliness which ought to characterize the children of God" (*My Utmost for His Highest*, 159). This doesn't mean that there won't be storms in the center of God's will. Problems arise there too. But in the midst of them, there will be a simple and quiet peace that passes all understanding.

The will of God is greater than any one detail of our lives. If we miss the mark a few times, it doesn't forever sentence us to living outside God's best. If you know you've missed the mark by walking in rebellion, put every area of your life back into submission to the Lord. By His grace He'll get you back on target.

Reject the Pitfall of Rejection

My earliest memory of rejection is of being locked in that closet by my mother. Had it been an isolated incident, it might not have been so bad. But it wasn't. As a result, I grew up feeling rejected, and the feelings of rejection grew in me until no amount of affirmation and encouragement could overcome them.

I became an overachiever to gain approval. I worked hard so that people would notice me and say I did a good job. When they did, the good feeling only lasted for the moment. I was certain that if people really knew the truth about me and my limitations, they would not have such a favorable opinion. I expected rejection.

Just a few years ago I ran into the best friend of a young man I had dated seriously when I was working in television. We talked briefly about old times together and, of course, my old boyfriend.

"Ron was devastated when you severed the relationship so abruptly," he told me.

"He was?" I asked in amazement. "I thought he didn't care that much and it was best that we just get on with our lives."

"Oh, no," the friend said, "he felt you were the girl for him. In fact, he planned to ask you to marry him that summer. He could never figure out why you walked out on the relationship."

I was shocked. It was not that I wished I had stayed with Ron or felt that I'd made a foolish mistake by leaving him, but I was amazed at how my feelings of rejection had blinded me.

The lie we believe when we feel rejection is, *I'm not worth anything, so it's completely understandable that people will reject me.* A spirit of rejection convinces you that you *will* be rejected, and then every word and action of other people is interpreted through the eyes of rejection.

Each of us has been rejected—by a family member, a friend, a teacher, a stranger, or a casual acquaintance. When we're emotionally healthy, such an incident won't set us back much. We are soon able to put it in perspective and get over it. But if we have deep emotional scars from repeated incidents of rejection, the smallest incident will feel like a knife to the heart.

Years after Michael and I were married, our relationship struck an impasse because of chronic miscommunication, so we searched for a qualified third person to help us.

"You've allowed a spirit of rejection to color everything you've heard each other say," our marriage counselor told us. "Every time one of you said or did something, a spirit of rejection interpreted it for the other. You both have to learn to relate to one another, not expecting rejection, but expecting acceptance and receiving it."

I had never thought of rejection as a spirit, but the more I pondered what the counselor told us, the more I began to identify that spirit rising up in me. I interpreted Michael's working long hours and being gone all the time as rejection of me. When he went golfing with his friends on his one day off, I interpreted that as rejection. When he was short with me, I interpreted it as rejection instead of attributing it to his being under pressure. My responses came out of my own feelings of rejection.

"Rejection is a spirit that has to be fed to stay alive," the counselor said, "and it has to be starved in order to kill it. It is fed and grows by believing negative thoughts about yourself. It is starved to death by refusing to give it the destructive food it wants and instead building and nourishing yourself on the love and acceptance of God.

"It's not that the power of this spirit is greater than the Lord's power to cast it out, but you can't be delivered from something you are giving place to. If you feed a stray dog, he's going to stay. If you are feeding a spirit of rejection, it's going to stay also. The best way to starve a spirit of rejection is to fill yourself with the knowledge of God's acceptance."

He sent us home with an assignment to find all the verses in the Bible about God's acceptance. We compiled a long list over the next few weeks. By the sixth and final week of our counseling, we had a much deeper understanding of God's love and how to receive it. The counselor prayed for each of us to be released from the spirit of rejection. Our relationship was renewed, and each of us found healing in our own souls.

Living Like a Chosen One

God said, "I chose you out of the world" (John 15:19). We did not choose Jesus first; He chose *us*. We must learn to live like the chosen ones we are.

When you sense the red light of rejection flashing off and on in your brain over some word or action someone has said or done, remember that Jesus chose *you*. Remember, too, that *the voice of God always encourages; the voice of the devil always discourages.* If you can't see anything good about yourself, it's because the devil has covered up your future with the past.

What the Bible Says About Rejection

I have chosen you and have not cast you away:
Fear not, for I am with you; be not dismayed,
for I am your God. I will strengthen you, Yes,
I will help you, I will uphold you with My
righteous right hand.

—Isaiah 41:9–10

For the LORD will not reject his people;
he will never forsake his inheritance.

—Psalm 94:14 NIV

For you are a holy people to the LORD your God;
the LORD your God has chosen you to be a
people for Himself.

—Deuteronomy 7:6

God from the beginning chose you for salvation
through sanctification by the Spirit and belief in
the truth.

—2 Thessalonians 2:13

For the LORD will not forsake His people, for
His great name's sake, because it has pleased the
LORD to make you His people.

—1 Samuel 12:22

Every time you feel rejection in any way, refuse to accept it. No matter how much your flesh wants to agree with it, say, "Spirit of rejection, I reject *you!* God accepts me and loves me just the way I am. Even if no one else on earth can accept me that way, I know that *He* does. I refuse to live in the pain of rejection any longer. I have been chosen by God, and I choose to live in His full acceptance. Thank You, God, for loving me. Praise You, God, for transforming me into all You made me to be."

Open up to God's love and acceptance and accept it for yourself. Your emotional health depends on it.

Reject the Pitfall of Self-Pity

People who have been emotionally damaged early on in life often end up negatively self-focused. The lie that plays over and over in their minds is, *Poor me. The worst things always happen to me.* When you rehearse misery day after day, you open yourself up to an evil spirit. This spirit of self-pity makes you feel bad for yourself *all the time* about *everything.* The smallest negative incident, like losing your car keys or spraining your ankle, becomes a sign that God is not on your side. You even continue to feel badly about things from which you have already been set free.

Oswald Chambers said, "Beware of allowing self-consciousness to continue because by slow degrees it will awaken self-pity and self-pity is Satanic" (*My Utmost for His Highest,* 170). Self-pity is a work of the devil, who is intent upon stealing life away from you to destroy you. Remember that. It may seem right to be sorry for yourself because of bad things that happened, but allowing yourself to feel that way all the time means you are ignoring the power of God in your life now. And that's exactly what Satan wants. Self-pity keeps you forever from moving into all God has for you.

What the Bible Says About Self-Pity

I have been crucified with Christ; it is no
longer I who live, but Christ lives in me;
and the life which I now live in the flesh I
live by faith in the Son of God, who loved me
and gave Himself for me.

—*Galatians 2:20*

For godly sorrow produces repentance leading
to salvation, not to be regretted; but the sorrow
of the world produces death.

—*2 Corinthians 7:10*

Test yourselves. Do you not know yourselves,
that Jesus Christ is in you?

—*2 Corinthians 13:5*

But you, beloved, building yourselves up on
your most holy faith, praying in the Holy
Spirit, keep yourselves in the love of God,
looking for the mercy of our Lord Jesus
Christ unto eternal life.

—*Jude 20—21*

Whoever has no rule over his own spirit
Is like a city broken down, without walls.

—*Proverbs 25:28*

Focusing on God

Self-pity keeps us focused entirely on ourselves. The opposite of focusing *inward* on self is focusing *outward* on God. Oswald Chambers said, "The initiative of the saint is not towards self-realization, but towards knowing Jesus Christ" (*My Utmost for His Highest*, 140). How opposite this is from what the world promotes today! We mistakenly think that an intense focus on ourselves will contribute most to our happiness and fulfillment, when actually the opposite is true. Dwelling on ourselves leads to emotional sickness. *Instead of being filled with thoughts about what we need and feel, we must be full of thoughts of the Lord.*

Our complete focus must be on God alone. The Bible says, "The backslider in heart will be filled with his own ways, but a good man will be satisfied from above" (Prov. 14:14). The best way to focus on God is to thank Him continually for all He has given, praise Him for all He has done, and worship Him for all He is. It's impossible to be self-focused with self-pity while you are glorifying God in that way.

Also, resolve that you will not sin with your mind or your mouth. Say aloud, "I refuse to sit around thinking about what I need and want and feel. I refuse to mourn and moan about the past, present, and future. I deliberately choose to think about only You, Lord, and Your goodness. I look to You to meet all my needs. You know what they are even better than I do."

Deliberately avoid the pitfall of self-pity by focusing on the Lord in thanksgiving and praise to your Creator. Your emotional health depends on it.

Reject the Pitfall of Suicide

When I was fourteen I was so overcome with emotional torment that I could not envision a future. I felt ugly, worthless, stupid, unwanted, and unloved, especially by my parents. One night when I had done nothing to provoke it, my mother unleashed a venomous verbal attack, accusing me of things I had not done. I was helpless to defend myself against her rage, and I suffered such extreme loneliness, depression, and hopelessness that I felt crushed and emotionally mutilated. I saw no possibility for things ever to be any different, and I decided I didn't want to live. I took an overdose of drugs that night, but it was not to attract attention or make people feel sorry for me. I didn't leave a note or phone for help. I simply did not want to wake up again.

The first lie we believe when we contemplate suicide is, *There is no way out.* We believe that our situation is hopeless. Then we accept the lie that death is the only means of escape. In the Lord, these things are *never* true, no matter how painful and agonizing your circumstances. God *in* you is stronger than anything you are facing, and with Him comes freedom and deliverance.

The Torment of Suicidal Thoughts

Nearly everyone with any serious emotional damage will at one time or another consider suicide. If that ever happens to you, remember that those thoughts come from Satan. A desire to die is not from God and is not from you. You may want to be free of physical and emotional pain, and rightly so, but the thought of killing yourself to do it comes from a spirit of death sent from hell to destroy you. *It is not you!* The Spirit of God in you *always* has a solution that leads to life.

If you are contemplating suicide, as I know some who read these pages may be, I want to tell you that I have been in the same bottomless pit you're in, and I've known the anguish, despair, and pain. I've heard and believed the same lies of the devil saying:

- "Death would be better. Go ahead and do it."
- "End this agony. Put a stop to this emptiness."
- "Don't worry about what it would do to anyone else. Nobody really cares anyway. Actually, you'll be doing them a favor."
- "You can't live with this pain another moment. Get it over with and kill yourself now."

I know that many people think of suicide as selfish—and it *is* the final act of a person focused intently upon self—-but I know from experience that when you're suicidal, something beyond selfishness overtakes you. I know that down deep you really *do* want to live, but you don't want to live the way you've been living. A voice in your mind tells you you'd be better off dead. You really do want to have hope, but you have a voice telling you it's hopeless. And because you're mentally tormented and emotionally weak at the moment, you believe it. But the truth is, *you want to live.*

Fortunately I didn't take enough drugs to do the job when I was fourteen, so I ended up sick instead of dead. When I did wake up, however, I felt different, even though nothing in my circumstances had changed. I wasn't sure why I had been spared from death, but somehow I didn't feel like dying anymore. Why my perception changed, I don't know. Perhaps someone prayed for me, although I never knew of anyone who did. But for some reason only God knows, my life was spared and I felt differently. I felt like fighting back, and I decided to do it by taking steps to get out of my miserable situation.

That's why it's important to remember, even in the midst of suicidal thoughts, that *at any moment in our lives, things can change.* In fact, change is inevitable. The only thing that doesn't change is God: "For I am the LORD, I do not change" (Mal. 3:6). God is always working on your behalf. *You may feel like killing yourself now, but tomorrow afternoon you could feel entirely different.*

Resisting Thoughts of Suicide

A suicidal spirit gains control over you when you say, "I don't want to live any more" a few times to yourself. That invites an all-too-willing spirit of death in to assist you in fulfilling that desire to escape life. And don't think that because you have received Jesus you can get away with those thoughts either. No matter when you say you want to die, a spirit of suicide is happy to accommodate you.

Whether you feel suicidal at this moment or not, you need to confess before the Lord any time in your life that you ever said or thought that you wanted to die. After you do that, then say aloud: "I recognize the desire to die as coming from you, Satan, and I renounce you in Jesus' name. I refuse your lying spirit and the only truth I accept is the truth of God, which says His plans and purposes for me are for good. Therefore my future is not hopeless. I want to live and glorify my Father God. By the authority given to me in Jesus' name, I smash the spirit of suicide and refuse any voice that tells me I deserve to die. Thank You, Jesus, that *You* died to break every hold death wants to have on my life."

If you have to say this prayer twenty times a day, do it. I was freed from a spirit of suicide in the counseling office with

Mary Anne, so I was never gripped by it again. However, several times since I have come to the Lord, I have been taunted by that spirit. But when I said that prayer, the thoughts left. Don't give the spirit of suicide a place for even one moment.

Once you renounce wanting to die, you will have to deal with why you wanted to die in the first place. You may need to forgive certain people for what they have done, or God for what you think He should have done, or yourself for not being what *you* think you should be. Be sure to confess anything that needs to be confessed so you can receive God's full forgiveness toward you.

Never attempt to handle serious suicidal thoughts without help. Seek out someone who can counsel you now. A Christian psychologist would be best, but if you can't get to one, try a suicide hotline, a psychiatrist, a pastor, a counselor, a friend, or a strong believer in the Lord. Get together with other believers who can pray with you and for you, and make sure you go to church regularly for extensive times of worship and prayer. You must be built up from the inside.

The Best Is Yet to Come

Pastor Jack always taught us that the best part of our lives is ahead. In the twenty years I've walked with Jesus, that has proven true. That little girl who spent so much time locked in the closet now has a loving husband who provides well for his family, children who love the Lord, and a fulfilling and fruitful life. I never imagined these blessings, *especially* when I was contemplating suicide. Had I carried out my suicide plans, I never would have experienced any of it.

It doesn't matter whether you can see it or even imagine it at the moment, God has great things in store for you. Jesus said, "I have come that they may have life, and that they may have it more abundantly" (John 10:10). You have to take it on faith. You have to know that there is no pit so deep that Jesus can't pull you out. The devil *has* blinded you. God has *not* forsaken you. Things *always* change. God is able to transform your circumstances, and this may be the time. If you kill yourself, you will never know the wonderful things that He has waiting for you. Why miss the greatest part of your life by ending it? Know that because Jesus lives, your life *is* worth living too.

Prayer

Lord, I pray that You would deliver my feet from the snares of the enemy, and my soul from the torment and death he has prepared for me. Hide me in the shadow of Your wings. Be my fortress, shield, and strength. Give me discernment. Open my eyes to the truth. May I be quick to recognize the errors of my own thoughts. I submit my life to You. Lead me in the way You would have me to go.

What the Bible Says About
Rejecting the Pitfalls

There is a way which seems right to a man,
But its end is the way of death.

—Proverbs 14:12

For they have dug a pit to take me,
And hidden snares for my feet.

—Jeremiah 18:22

And he who comes up from the midst of
the pit shall be caught in the snare.

—Isaiah 24:18

The fear of the LORD is a fountain of life, to
turn one away from the snares of death.

—Proverbs 14:27 NIV

For You have delivered my soul from death,
my eyes from tears, and my feet from
falling. I will walk before the LORD in the
land of the living.

—Psalm 116:8—9

STEP SEVEN: STAND STRONG

When the phone rang, I leaped to answer it. Diane's tests were due to be back, and we would find out what had been causing her pain and failure to recover from what we thought must be a bad case of the flu. Since we'd met in drama class in high school twenty-eight years before, we'd been best friends. We quickly discovered how much we had in common, including our similar family situations. After I received Jesus, I led her to the Lord and she started coming to church with me every Sunday. We became steady prayer partners, praying four or five times a week together on the phone. In those years I did not make an important decision without her prayers.

Two years prior to this phone call, she discovered she had breast cancer. After having both breasts removed, she'd been found cancer-free at each checkup. Still we always were concerned that it might come back.

"Stormie," the voice on the other end of the line sounded uncharacteristically small and shaken.

"What did the doctor say?"

"It's not good—" Her voice broke.

"What do you mean? What happened on the tests?"

"The cancer is back."

"Back where?" I held my breath in anticipation of the answer.

"It's everywhere—in my glands, my stomach, my bones, possibly my brain."

"Oh, dear Jesus, help us," I said as we both broke into tears. I don't know how many seconds or minutes passed with just the sound of muffled sobs. When we could talk again, we discussed her eight-year-old son, John.

"I just want to see him grow up," she cried.

We talked about the treatment the doctor had suggested for her. The megadoses of chemotherapy and radiation she described sounded like a death sentence. We prayed together for a miracle from God.

This happened in June, and during the summer months that followed, John stayed with us while his father took care of Diane. She suffered terribly, always growing weaker and more miserable, and by September 13 she was gone. Of course, we all knew she was with the Lord, but the loss was great.

The grief seemed unbearable to me. During Diane's decline and in the months after her death, I struggled with my own physical problems (caused, no doubt, by the serious mistreatment of my body in my early twenties), which resulted in a total hysterectomy. A few weeks after the surgery, we sold our house and business, packed up, moved to a new location, and built a new studio. Then an unforeseen turn of events in the music business put us under severe financial strain, which in turn inflicted tremendous strain on our marriage. Dealing with all of these difficulties at once left me physically and emotionally drained.

"God, it feels as if my life is coming to an end," I cried to the Lord one night. "What can replace these losses? Why won't this sadness over Diane's death go away? I can't function well with it. And, God, help Michael and me. We're not living the way You want us to in our relationship. And did we hear You right about buying the house and building a new studio? We prayed for a year about it, and I thought we were clearly directed by You. All this is overwhelming, Lord, and I can't handle it anymore."

"Good. Now let *Me* take this burden for you," I heard the Lord instruct my heart. "You just stand strong in all you know of My truth, and I will take care of everything."

In spite of this word of comfort from God, that whole season was like being in a terrible storm. As the winds tossed the branches of my life, I held tight to my roots, just as He said. I lived with a sense of purpose, no matter how I ached inside or how shaky things felt around me. I stayed in the Word, I prayed, I praised, I surrendered more of myself and my life to Him, I lived God's way even when I felt like giving up. When the storm was over and I was still standing, I knew more than ever that I had chosen solid ground upon which to grow.

Eventually things turned around. I received healing from my grief over Diane's death as God gave me deeper relationships with others and with Him. I recovered from the hysterectomy and felt better than I had in years. Miracles happened in my husband's business, our studio and house were saved, and our marriage became stronger than ever. It sounds as if I should say I lived happily ever after, but the truth is that all this could just as easily have gone the other direction. My life could have been washed away by bankruptcy, divorce, and emotional and physical sickness. These kinds of things happen to good people all the time. But I hung on to the Lord, and not only did I get through it, I came out stronger. Only God can bring us back from hell and make us better for it. *But the key was standing strong in Him and doing what was right, no matter what.*

Trusting God for Every Step

If we are to have total deliverance, total wholeness, and total restoration, there comes a time when we have to stand up and say, "This is what I believe; this is the way I will live; this is what I will and will not accept—and that's the way it is." We have to decide to stand strong and do what we know is right to do no matter what happens around us. Oswald Chambers said, "An average view of the Christian life is that it means deliverance from trouble. It is deliverance *in* trouble, which is very different" (*My Utmost for His Highest,* 157).

The Bible doesn't say we won't have problems. In fact, it says quite the opposite: "Many are the afflictions of the righteous, but the LORD delivers him out of them all" (Ps. 34:19). We don't need to fear because God uses our problems for good when we commit them to prayer and are obedient to His ways. Bad things do happen to good people. God never said they wouldn't. He didn't say life is fair. He said *He* is fair, and He will bring life out of our problems.

Growing Up in the Lord

One of the last times I saw Mary Anne before she moved away, I went to her for some problem that I don't even remember now. What I *do* remember was her wise counsel, which amounted to two words: "Grow up," she said lovingly.

"What?" I asked.

"It's time to grow up, Stormie," she repeated in her patient voice. When my mother screamed those words at me for years, it felt like a beating. When Mary Anne said them, it felt like the Holy Spirit.

"Grow up?" I repeated, hoping for more details.

"Yes, Stormie. You need to get alone with the Lord and ask *Him* the questions you're asking *me*. Then you tell me what He's saying to you."

Everything she said felt right to me, and I laughed about it later when I told Michael. "You've got to admit that when you go to a counselor for help and she tells you to grow up, it's a sign of emotional health if you can see how funny that is."

I did ask the Lord, just as she said, and I did hear the answer, just as she predicted. It was then I knew without a doubt that I had everything I needed for my life right within me. I just had to stand strong in the Lord. I walked a little taller after that.

A point comes in our walk with the Lord when we've had enough teaching, enough counseling, enough deliverance, and enough knowledge of God's ways to be able to stand on our own two feet and say, "I am not going to live on the negative side of life any more." We can't depend on someone to hold our hand and make difficult times go away. We have to "grow up" and take responsibility for our lives. We have to decide we won't be the victims of our circumstances because God has given us a way out. We are not to stand in our own power. We must stand strong in Him.

"Let the weak say, 'I am strong,'" the Bible says (Joel 3:10). This does not mean you say, "I think I can" or "Maybe I'll try." You say, "This is it. I will stand firm in the Lord. I will stand strong against the enemy. I will not cry, complain, and lament over what isn't. I will rejoice over what is and all that God is doing." This means standing strong in what you know and in whom you trust. It means growing up, and that's what emotional health is all about.

Standing Strong When the Enemy Attacks

There will be times when you are doing everything you know to do and things are going well, and then suddenly depression will cloud your mind or low self-esteem will dominate your actions. Or unforgiveness will return in full force, or all hell will break loose in a relationship. Or you'll have problems in an area where you've found deliverance and healing. Suddenly things will seem worse than they have ever been. This means that you are under an attack from the devil. Don't be frightened. It happens to everybody at one time or another.

At those times you have to understand without a doubt that *when you walk with Jesus, you never walk backward.* God has made it clear in His Word that if we have our eyes on Him, we will go from glory to glory and strength to strength. The apostle Paul told the Corinthians, "But we all, with unveiled face, beholding as in a mirror the glory of the Lord, are being transformed into the same image from glory to glory, just as by the Spirit of the Lord" (2 Cor. 3:18). And the psalmist tells us, "They go from strength to strength, each one appears before God in Zion" (Ps. 84:7).

To go backward, you would have to deliberately turn your back on God and walk in the other direction. As long as you are looking to Him, you are moving forward. It does not matter how it *feels;* that's the way it is.

Don't get confused. God is on *your* side. He is not responsible for the tragic death of a loved one, the divorce, the husband who drinks, the loss of your job, the accident, the strife in your family, the illness, the feelings of inadequacy. Satan is responsible. Satan is your enemy and wants you to believe his lies. He comes to you at your weakest (especially physically) and mixes his lies with just enough truth that you believe them.

Along with the grief over my friend's death came a sudden frightening feeling that I would die too. I had so closely identified with her for twenty-eight years that her death made life seem extremely fragile and fleeting. I was gripped by that thought until one Sunday morning during church worship, as I was voicing praise and thanksgiving to God for the life He had given me, I saw clearly I had been under satanic attack. I was weak physically and emotionally. The devil had bombarded my mind with the thought that my mother had died of cancer, that my best friend who was my age had died of cancer, and that therefore I could soon die of cancer too.

During that church service God presented me with the *whole* truth: I'm not my mother, nor am I Diane. If God chooses to call me home, it will not be on the basis of what happened to them. It will be in *His* timing. Tears of joy welled up as I thanked God for my life with renewed hope.

This story is just one small incident of many that you or I or any other believer could tell of enemy attack. If you recognize that this kind of attack has happened to you, don't let the devil push you around. If he has kept you in poverty or sickness or tragedy upon tragedy, stand up with courage, knowing that God has given you authority over him. Yes, we do have times of suffering. But they do not go on and on. And when the Lord is attending the suffering, you become stronger in Him.

Four Ways to Recognize Enemy Attack

When God is working in your life, things that you are attached to are being shaken loose, and parts of your flesh are being crucified. This doesn't feel good. But neither does the attack of the devil. The only way you can know for sure which is happening is to let the Spirit of God reveal it to you through His Word. You do that by spending time in His presence in praise and worship and prayer. Say, "Is this You, God, or is this the devil?" He will show you.

Too many people assume that they deserve everything that's happening to them. They don't suspect that it might be a shot directed at them from enemy territory. That's why it's important to know how to identify the enemy's attack.

I don't want to reduce everything to steps and formulas, but sometimes we need simple guidelines. Often the attack is of such magnitude that we can hardly see straight, let alone figure out clear direction for ourselves. This is especially true of anyone who has been abused or rejected. Because Satan will always attack your self-worth, you can be shaken violently. With that in mind, I have four suggestions that will help you navigate those rough times.

1. *Know God well enough to understand His heart.* If I had not been so exhausted emotionally and physically in the year of Diane's suffering and death, I would have recognized the voice of the devil more quickly. But in my weakened state, I listened. Looking back, I wonder why I thought God would say to me, "Your mother and your best friend died of cancer; you're going to die that way too." This does not sound like the voice of God. The realization of that truth came to me when I was in the Lord's presence.

Soon after this happened, a friend called to tell me her young son was very ill and asked if it might be the Lord punishing her for not being in church.

"You don't understand the heart of the Lord, Mary," I countered. "The Lord doesn't make someone sick, and He certainly never punishes us for things we neglect to do by allowing something to happen to our children. These thoughts are from the devil, and he's the one we need to battle. You're assured victory over his attack when you depend on God. In fact, you can't lose."

Make sure that your knowledge of the Lord and your desire for His presence is so strong that you won't give the devil any ground. Satan will always try to push your back to the wall, but don't let him. Push *his* back to the wall by saying, "I will *not* allow defeat! My God is my defender and I refuse you entry into my life."

Get clear in your mind the things that are always true about God, and hold them alongside what is happening in your life to see if they line up. Mary's fear that God was punishing her for not going to church does not line up with God's goodness. Don't focus on what's going on *around* you, but rather who's *in* you. I've included a list of things that are always true about God. Say them over and over again when you are tempted by the devil.

2. *Know who Satan is.* You may be thinking, *I don't want any part of a battle with the devil. In fact, I prefer not to even think about things like that.* Yet God and Satan are in a battle for your life. The war is real, and denying it will not change that reality. If you are a believer, you're already on the side that wins. But if you aren't where you're supposed to be (in God's will, in His presence, in His truth, in obedience to Him), then you've come out from under His covering, and you can get shot down in the crossfire. People who lose the battle often do so because they believe victory just happens. It doesn't. We must identify the enemy and the battle lines and make sure we're marching in the right army.

Seven Things I Know Are True About God

1. *I know that God is a good God.*
   "Good and upright is the LORD"
   (Ps. 25:8).

2. *I know that God is on my side.*
   "The LORD is on my side" (Ps. 118:6).
   "God is for me" (Ps. 56:9).

3. *I know that God's laws and ways are for my benefit.*
   "The judgments of the LORD are true and righteous altogether . . . And in keeping them there is great reward" (Ps. 19:9, 11).

4. *I know that God is always with me.*
   "I will never leave you nor forsake you" (Heb. 13:5).

5. *I know that God wants me restored.*
   "For You have delivered my soul from death"
   (Ps. 116:8).

6. *I know that God's promises to me will*
   never fail.
   "Your faithfulness endures to all generations"
   (Ps. 119:90).

7. *I know that God is always the winner.*
   "He shall prevail against His enemies"
   (Isa. 42:13).

If you doubt any of these statements, read the
entire chapter from which the Scripture below
it was taken, and ask God to make the truth of
His promise real to your heart.

As I was worshiping the Lord that day in church, I realized again that *Satan* was my enemy and *he* wanted me dead. I could now see how *he* had been relentlessly trying to undermine what God was doing in my life. I remembered that *he* is the loser, not God, and *I* am the winner because I belong to the Lord.

Learn the truth about the devil so that you are constantly aware of the nature of his intentions. The statements about the devil that I include in this chapter are true.

Sometimes we blame ourselves for what's happening. If we are sick or poor or have some bad things happen to us, we think it's all our fault. Yet there is a difference between taking responsibility for your life and blaming yourself for everything. Sometimes we have met the enemy, and it is *not* us. One of Satan's plans is to keep people weighed down with guilt over things *he* is doing. He disguises himself and sometimes even comes to you as *you*. At least you *believe* it's you. You have to remember that the devil is out to crush you whenever he can, and you must decide whether you will go along with his plans or not.

3. *Know what makes you most susceptible to satanic attack.* Often we give Satan unintentional invitations to attack us by what we do or don't do. For example, during those weeks after Diane died, I became so worn out emotionally and physically that I neglected to spend much time with the Lord. I felt too tired to read more than a verse or two of Scripture a day. Because I had lost my dear prayer partner, I prayed much less than I had when she was alive. I had a constant lump in my throat over her death, and I didn't feel like praising God nearly as much. I went to church regularly, but I was not in fellowship with other believers. It was a

Seven Things I Know Are
True About the Devil

1. *I know that Satan is my enemy.*
   "For we do not wrestle against flesh and blood, but against principalities, against powers, against the rulers of the darkness of this age, against spiritual hosts of wickedness in the heavenly places" (Eph. 6:12).

2. *I know that Satan robs, kills, and destroys.*
   "The thief does not come except to steal, and to kill, and to destroy" (John 10:10).

3. *I know that Satan is a deceiver.*
   "When he speaks a lie, he speaks from his own resources, for he is a liar and the father of it" (John 8:44).

4. *I know that Satan disguises himself.*
   "For Satan himself transforms himself into an angel of light" (2 Cor. 11:14).

5. *I know that Satan never rests from doing evil.*

   "Be sober, be vigilant; because your adversary the devil walks about like a roaring lion, seeking whom he may devour" (1 Peter 5:8).

6. *I know that Satan will always try to undermine what God does in my life.*

   "When they hear, Satan comes immediately and takes away the word that was sown in their hearts" (Mark 4:15).

7. *I know that Satan is a loser.*

   "Now is the judgment of this world; now the ruler of this world will be cast out" (John 12:31).

If you doubt any of these statements, look up the Scripture and read the entire chapter from which it was taken. Ask God to make its truth real to your heart.

time when my life was about to make a new beginning in every area (marriage, friendship, writing, finances), but I just couldn't see it. In fact, I saw just the opposite. I felt my life was over. Yet because I was in church when I was supposed to be, God made His truth alive to my heart and revealed the enemy's attack to me.

We can fend off much enemy attack by simply paying attention to the reasons he gains access to our lives. Take an inventory of your life by checking any area in which you are weak:

Seven Reasons the Enemy Can Attack

○ I have neglected to read the Word, God's truth, so I have no frame of reference for detecting a lie.

○ I have neglected to pray, so I have lost all power.

○ I haven't spent time in praise and worship, so I have forfeited the opportunity for God's presence to dwell powerfully in my life.

○ I have not lived in all the ways of the Lord, so my enemy has found an entry point.

○ I am due for a major breakthrough of some kind in an area of my life, but I struggle with doubt that it could actually happen for me.

○ I am walking in disobedience in regard to something God has specifically directed me to do.

○ I am moving out in a new area or dimension of ministry and have not sought prayer covering.

What the Bible Says About Standing Strong When the Enemy Attacks

Blessed is the man who endures temptation; for when he has been approved, he will receive the crown of life which the Lord has promised to those who love Him.

—James 1:12

When the storm has swept by, the wicked are gone, but the righteous stand firm forever.

—Proverbs 10:25 NIV

Resist him, standing firm in the faith, because you know that your brothers throughout the world are undergoing the same kind of sufferings.

—1 Peter 5:9 NIV

Escape the snare of the devil, having been taken captive by him to do his will.

—2 Timothy 2:26

He delivered me from my strong enemy.

—Psalm 18:17

If you checked any of the statements on page 213, confess it to God, and ask Him to show you what to do about it.

4. *Know the signs of satanic attack.* If you learn to recognize the signs of satanic attack, you will be better able to establish your own defense and to counterattack. If you don't you may end up aiding the enemy. The devil can attack you through your mind, your emotions, your body, your relationships, or your circumstances. If you can immediately recognize negative emotions such as fear, guilt, depression, confusion, and lack of peace as coming from the enemy, instead of accepting them as truth, you can protect yourself better. See if any of these seven signs of satanic attack are threatening you:

Seven Signs of Satanic Attack

○ I experience sudden, paralyzing fear that leaves me incapacitated.

○ I have guilt that is overwhelming and doesn't respond to confession or a corrected walk.

○ I have recurring depression or depression that lasts a long time.

○ I have what feels like hell breaking loose in my mind, body, emotions, or situation, especially in an area where there has already been deliverance.

○ I have no peace about specific things that are happening to me.

○ I have great confusion at a point where I once had clarity.

○ I am receiving ideas in my mind that are in direct opposition to God's ways.

If you have checked any one of the previous statements, pray that this attack of Satan be stopped. Praying with one or more believers about this is also very important.

What to Do When the Enemy Attacks

When you first sense you are under enemy attack, go immediately back to the basics.

1. *Check to see that you are proclaiming the Lordship of Jesus in every area of your life.* Sometimes we exclude Him without realizing it. Say, "Jesus is Lord over my mind." "Jesus is Lord over my finances." "Jesus is Lord over my relationships." "Jesus is Lord over my health." Specifically name the area the enemy is threatening.

2. *Saturate yourself with God's Word.* Read especially any promises from God concerning this specific type of enemy attack, and speak them aloud in the face of your circumstances. You can go back to the list of pitfalls in the last chapter and refer to the Scriptures in areas that apply to you.

3. *Be much in prayer.* Ask God to reveal the truth of your situation to you. Ask Him for guidance, protection, and strength for whatever you are facing. Remember: there is no unity in the realm of darkness. That's why the two weakest Christians have more power, if they are in unity, than all the power of hell.

4. *Continue to praise God in the midst of whatever is happening.* Remember God inhabits the praises of His people, and you will always be safe in His presence.

5. *Ask God to show you if there are any points of obedience that you have not taken.* Lack of obedience always opens us up to enemy attack.

6. *Fast and pray.* This is a powerful weapon for breaking down enemy strongholds that have been erected against you.

7. *Resist Satan.* Don't run from the enemy, but instead face him with all the spiritual weapons at your disposal. Because of Jesus in you, you have full authority and power over Satan.

8. *Rest in the Lord.* Once you have done all you know to do, be still and know that Jesus is the victor and the battle is the Lord's. Gain strength in that knowledge.

When the heat is on and the battle is raging, know that as long as you are standing strong in the Lord, you won't be shot down or burned up by your circumstances. If it looks like all hell is breaking loose in your life, know God will bring heaven to rule in your situation. *Think in terms of God's power and not your own weakness.* Don't give the devil the pleasure of seeing you give up.

Standing Strong When Your Prayers Haven't Been Answered

There will be times that your prayers will not be answered—at least not exactly the way you prayed them or according to your timetable. If that happens, trust that God knows what is best.

Until Diane died, I and all who knew her never stopped praying for her healing. Hundreds of strong believers in two different congregations prayed for her continually. If her healing depended on prayer and faith, she was covered. But those specific prayers were not answered, at least not the way we wanted them to be.

We all have lived through the painful consequences of unanswered prayer. Sometimes what seems like unanswered prayer is actually a matter of waiting on God. Other times the prayers are answered so differently from what we expect that we can't even see they've been answered until much later. Sometimes our prayers are never answered at all as we have prayed them. The key is standing strong in the Lord whether we see that our prayers are answered or not.

When getting an answer to prayer takes a long time, we sometimes lose hope. We become discouraged and fear the Lord has forgotten us. We stop praying, stop going to church, stop reading the Bible, stop obeying God's rules because we think *What's the point?* Sometimes we get mad at God. We don't like waiting the two weeks, two months, two years, or as long as it takes for the answer to come. And what if the answer never comes? That's miserable and we don't like to suffer.

The Purpose of Suffering

Everyone, without exception, suffers at one time or another. No one is exempt. Sometimes we do stupid or sinful things that lead to misery. Sometimes it's satanic attack. Sometimes we suffer because we are not doing what God is directing us to do. Sometimes people think that if there is no *immediate* suffering when they stray from God's ways, they are getting away with something. Later on, when they're miserable, they don't connect the two.

Sometimes suffering is used by God to refine us. He does not put the suffering upon us, but He allows us to be in it for our own purifying. And no matter how hard we pray, there is still a season of it in our lives because through it His purposes are worked in us.

No one suffers willingly. Even Jesus asked God for His suffering on the cross to be eliminated if at all possible. The good news is that what comes out of suffering is so far above what we endure that it more than compensates for our misery: "The sufferings of this present time are not worthy to be compared with the glory which shall be revealed in us" (Rom. 8:18). God is not minimizing our suffering in that Scripture; He's putting it in perspective. The great things ahead for those who stand strong are so far superior to what we can imagine that our suffering will seem momentary when weighed against the entirety of our lives here on earth.

I was miserably sick throughout both of my pregnancies. I have never before or since experienced such physical suffering and have no desire to repeat it. But the rewards of having my son and daughter are so superior to my suffering that I can't even compare the two. Even knowing that my prayers for an easy pregnancy would not be answered, I would still choose to go through it again.

When you feel your prayers are not answered, God reveals two things to you: *His grace and His power*. His grace sustains and keeps you, and His power delivers you. God wants us to see without a doubt that *we are limited* in our power. He also wants us to see that *He is not*. He sometimes waits until all hope outside of Him is dead so that we will know it is He who brought life where there was none. Sometimes He takes things out of our lives so that we will turn to Him to supply our need. No matter how much God blesses us, He wants us to acknowledge that we depend on Him. He uses the storms of our lives to accomplish that purpose.

What the Bible Says About Standing Strong When Your Prayers Haven't Been Answered

Beloved, do not think it strange concerning
the fiery trial which is to try you, as though
some strange thing happened to you;
but rejoice to the extent that you partake of
Christ's sufferings, that when His glory
is revealed, you may also be glad with exceeding joy.

—1 Peter 4:12–13

In this you greatly rejoice, though now for a
little while, if need be, you have been grieved
by various trials, that the genuineness of your
faith, being much more precious than gold that
perishes, though it is tested by fire, may be
found to praise, honor, and glory at the revelation of Jesus Christ.

—1 Peter 1:6–7

But may the God of all grace, who called us to
His eternal glory by Christ Jesus, after you
have suffered a while, perfect, establish,
strengthen, and settle you.

—1 Peter 5:10

Treasures of Darkness

God is God when things are bad as well as when they are good, when it is dark as well as when it is light. Sometimes the darkness around us is not a darkness of death but rather a darkness like in a womb, where we are growing and being made ready for birth. Just as a child in the womb knows nothing of the world waiting for him, so we do not realize the greatness of God's purpose for us. The Bible says, "I will give you the treasures of darkness" (Isa. 45:3). Certain valuable experiences in the Lord can *only* be found in the dark times.

When Diane died, her son, John David, was eight years old. Nearly eight years later, his father was killed in a car accident. John David, an only child, came to be part of our family because he was left to us in his father and mother's will. It was a dark time for all concerned, but we found a sense of the Lord's presence like never before.

Many of my closest encounters with the Lord have happened in these kinds of dark times when I turned to Him and found a more powerful presence of His Spirit than I had ever known. Those times have been precious, unforgettable, and life-changing. Through them I have found a larger portion of Him in me, and I wouldn't trade that now for anything.

Don't worry. This time of darkness, waiting, and unanswered prayer is not going to become a way of life. It's only a season of the soul.

How to Grow in the Dark

So what do you do when you've believed and praised and prayed but are still disillusioned and afraid your dreams and hopes are gone? First of all, don't be consumed with guilt. Don't feel that this is all your fault and therefore God won't answer your prayer. If your prayers are unanswered because of sin, confess it, stop doing it, and pray. God will turn things around.

Second, allow no situation to make you turn your back on Him. Know that He sees where you are, He has not forgotten you, and He will sustain you through it. Rest in the fact that He is in control and more powerful than your problems. It's at this time that we either turn away from the Lord's ways or determine to live them even more diligently. We can give up too soon and say, "This obviously isn't working so why bother doing it this way?" We can choose to try to ride the storm out by ourselves, or we can align with the God who either calms the storm or sets our feet on solid ground in the center of it where we won't be harmed. Far too many people have given up when the answer to their prayer was just around the corner.

Part of standing strong in times of unanswered prayer is waiting, and waiting produces patience. The Bible says, "In your patience possess your souls" (Luke 21:19). When you are patient, you're able to take control of your very being and place yourself in God's hands. He, then, is in control whether it is night or day in your soul. He becomes God to you in every season of your life—the good and the bad. And because you know Him that way, you become unshakable.

Since we have no choice but to wait, our attitude makes a lot of difference. We can either shake our fist at God and scream, "Why me?" Or we can open up our hearts to God and pray, "Lord, change this situation. Perfect Your life in me as I wait on You. Help me to do the right thing, and let it all work out for my greatest good."

You may have to wait for God to move, but you don't have to sit twiddling your thumbs until it happens. The best way to sustain a good attitude while you wait is to spend much time in praise and worship of God. Say, "Lord, I praise

You in the midst of this situation. I confess I'm afraid that my prayers may never be answered. I'm weary and discouraged from the waiting, and feel I'm losing the strength to fight. Forgive me, Lord, for not trusting You more. I pray my weariness would end and there would be renewed hope in my spirit. Help me to feel Your presence and Your love, and help me to hear Your voice and follow Your lead. Thank You that You are in full control."

Don't stop praying even if you've been doing it for a long time and it seems as if God must not be listening. God hears your every prayer. You may feel like nothing is going on, but you are tapping into God's love, healing, and redemption when you pray and surrender yourself and your life to Him daily.

Standing Strong When Your Prayers Have Been Answered

One of the big surprises for people who come out of the wilderness of their pasts and enter the promised land of answered prayer is that there are giants in the land and they have to fight against them in order to possess it. Because Satan never has a day when he is feeling friendly toward us, our prosperity, success, breakthrough, deliverance, and healing will not go unchallenged. We have to remember to stand strong against the work of the enemy in the easy times as well as the difficult.

During the year Diane died, Michael and I were finally brought to the realization that the devil had designed a plan to destroy our marriage, our business, and our health through our finances. Worse than that, we were allowing him to do it. Things had been going along well in the area of our finances, so we hadn't prayed much about them. Suddenly, they started to get very shaky. One evening, on the brink of what could have been financial ruin, Michael and I knelt before God and repented of our failure to cover our finances in prayer. We had not stopped tithing but had neglected to be prayerful about the stewardship of our income. We asked God to be in charge and bless us with restoration. *Every* morning we diligently prayed about it, and immediately the strain on our marriage and health showed signs of improvement. Soon the business and finances also began to turn around.

When a certain contract that we had been praying for came through, along with a large check, the pressure was off. We cheered, we praised God, we danced, we whooped, and we screamed. The very next day we slept later than usual, got up in a rush, and left the house before we had time to pray. The next few days brought situations that kept us from praying together as we had when things were tough. As it turned out, we were able to catch ourselves before disaster struck again, but our experience shows how we do not naturally turn to God when things are going well. And *we* knew better.

How Quickly We Forget

The truth about human flesh is that when we come to a place of comfort, we tend to forget God. As I read through the Old Testament from beginning to end, what impressed me most was how the Israelites sought God, repented, and prayed when things were bad, and God heard and answered their prayers. Once everything was going well, they forgot where they had come from, forgot what God had done, and starting living their own way again. In the tough times, they remembered God and did the right thing. In good times, they forgot God and sinned—time and again.

You and I are no different. How many of us can say that we pray as fervently when all is well as we do when all hell is breaking loose? Not many, I'm sure. If we could serve the Lord just as faithfully and fervently when our prayers *have* been answered as when they haven't, we might never have to suffer as we do. I'm not saying that life would be pain-free because life doesn't work that way, but we do sometimes suffer needlessly. The Bible says, "Let him who thinks he stands take heed lest he fall" (1 Cor. 10:12). When things are going well, beware!

Watch Out for the Giants

"The promised land the Bible talks about is a place of restoration," Mary Anne explained to me. "It's a time of renewing all that has been destroyed, stolen, or lost from our lives. When we enter the promised land, we don't think about the giants; we think about the milk and honey, about how good this feels and what life will be like now that we've been set free and are being renewed. We know that evil lurks about, but we don't want to think about that now, not when things are good. That's why when an attack comes, we are so unprepared. When we enter the promised land we need to know there are giants we must face."

"Who are these giants?" I asked.

Mary Anne named certain enemies that were in the promised land as described in the book of Exodus. She said she found that the meanings of their names correlated with areas of our flesh in which we struggle, such as fear, confusion, discouragement, pride, rebelliousness, and condemnation. These were exactly the ones that threatened me when I came into my time of restoration, and ones we must be ready to battle, even in time of peace.

Keep It Written in Stone

Years ago Pastor Jack instructed each family unit in our church, single or married, to go out and find a rock large enough to write the words, "As for me and my house, we will serve the LORD" (Josh. 24:15), and then put it in a prominent place in their home. Michael and I found a five-pound gray stone with a flat enough surface on one side to print that Scripture. We placed it next to the fireplace in the living room, and every time we see it, we remember our commitment to serve God and stand strong in Him. Everyone who comes in our house sees it, and I believe the devil knows it's there too. It's a good reminder for him—and for you.

I'm giving you an assignment. Go find yourself a decent-sized rock, print that Scripture on it with an indelible marker, and place it in the heart of your home. Whether you live in a one-room trailer, a forty-room mansion, or a corner of someone else's apartment, make sure those words are visible to you somewhere. It's a scriptural proclamation of where you stand, and it helps you to stand taller in the presence of giants.

Don't ever be fooled into believing that when all is going well, you don't need to read, pray, praise, and obey as carefully as you did before. Resolve to stand strong in the Lord, even when your prayers have been answered, and you will live safely in the promised land of God's restoration.

What the Bible Says About Standing Strong

Be strong in the Lord and in the
power of His might.

—Ephesians 6:10

By standing firm you will gain life.

—Luke 21:19 NIV

But you must continue in the things which
you have learned and been assured of, knowing from whom you have learned them.

—2 Timothy 3:14

Do not be deceived, God is not mocked; for
whatever a man sows, that he will also reap.
For he who sows to his flesh will of the
flesh reap corruption, but he who sows to
the Spirit will of the Spirit reap
everlasting life. And let us not grow weary
while doing good, for in due season we
shall reap if we do not lose heart.

—Galatians 6:7–9

Be steadfast, immovable, always abounding
in the work of the Lord, knowing that your
labor is not in vain in the Lord.

—1 Corinthians 15:58

BECOMING ALL GOD MADE YOU TO BE

*Y*ou've just gone through the Seven Steps to Emotional Health, and if you have taken even one step in each area, there are bound to be noticeable positive changes in your life. You may not see as many as you'd like yet, but don't give up. You will. God promises that "He who has begun a good work in you will complete it until the day of Jesus Christ" (Phil. 1:6).

I'm going to assume that if you've read this far, you've already decided you want all God has for you. This is good, because becoming all He created you to be begins with a deep desire in the heart. When that longing turns into a hunger for more of the Lord that can only be completely satisfied when you are in His presence, then you are on your way to becoming all you can be.

Now it's time to make your commitment to the Lord a solid one. It's time to start living what you believe and walking in the wholeness to which you plan to become accustomed. You'll be able to do that more effectively if you stay emotionally current and mindful of the truth about yourself.

Staying Emotionally Current

Once you are on the road to emotional health, remain sensitive to what is currently happening inside of you. That does not mean you sit around all day thinking about how you feel. The focus stays on Jesus. But now because your focus is so much on the Lord and living His way, you can deal with your emotions as they surface. In *The Road Less Traveled,* Scott Peck says, "Mental health is an ongoing process of dedication to reality at all costs" (New York: Simon and Schuster, 1980, 51). Covering up our emotions is the opposite.

Every one of us has countless tears buried inside. We've pulled back from crying because it didn't seem socially appropriate or because we were afraid that if we shed one tear, the floodgates would open and we wouldn't be able to regain control. Often there has been so much hurt we've had to harden our hearts to dull the pain. When we no longer feel the pain, we don't cry. This is a survival method, but it isn't healthy. The Bible says:

> To everything there is a season,
> A time for every purpose under heaven . . .
> A time to weep,
> And a time to laugh;
> A time to mourn,
> And a time to dance. (Eccl. 3:1, 4)

We would be wise to remember that.

I once heard a doctor say, "Colds are a result of uncried tears that back up and clog the system." I don't know if that can ever be scientifically proven, but I believe our emotions overflow onto our physical self more than we dream possible. We must stay current with our need to cry and feel free to let ourselves do it. Crying in the presence of the Lord brings much healing and should not be restricted.

Whatever has been lost to you must be mourned completely, whether it is the loss of a dream, a childhood, a part of your body, a marriage, a loved one, or a period of time in your life. Grief comes in stages, so don't let getting through one stage close you off to further stages. Each one is a different aspect of your loss. Don't avoid it out of fear. You won't be consumed by it; you will be released.

Our emotions don't have to rule our lives, but we shouldn't ignore them either. Part of letting go of the past involves facing the present. Listen to what you are feeling and ask God to help you identify it and deal with it. Get to the bottom of why you feel the way you do. Keep yourself emotionally current at all times.

Remembering the Truth About Yourself

"You're worthless! You're nothing! You're stupid! You're a failure! You're never going to amount to anything!" were words my mother used to say to me over and over again. They were reinforced by her lack of affection and inability to nurture. Because we lived on a ranch miles from anyone, I didn't have the positive reinforcement of friends or relatives, which could have lessened the impact of my mother's neglect. Every day I heard the same words, and I grew up believing them.

Since I believed I was nobody, I became desperate to prove I was somebody. I grabbed for things instead of letting them happen. I demanded approval. I had to be noticed. Starved for love, I became involved in one destructive relationship after another. Yet no amount of love, approval, or recognition ever filled the endless void of my being because I believed those lies about myself.

We all want to be somebody. The truth is, God created each one of us to be somebody and no life is an accident or unwanted in His eyes. He has given us *each* a distinct purpose or calling. It is not humility to deny the Lord's extraordinary qualities in us, it's low self-esteem.

High self-esteem means seeing yourself as God sees you, and recognizing that you are a unique person in whom He has placed specific gifts, talents, and purpose unlike anyone else. Memorize this, cut it out, paste it on your hand, and say it aloud fifty times a day. Do whatever it takes to help you remember it. This is the absolute truth about you, whether you can see it or not and whether or not anyone *else* recognizes it.

I have learned to value myself as God values me by deliberately thanking Him for any positive things I see. "Thank you, Lord, that I am alive, that I can walk, that I can talk, that I can see, that I can prepare a meal, that I can write letters, that I am neat, that I love my children, that I know Jesus. Thank you, God, that You have made me to be a person of worth and purpose." As we praise God for specific things, we are inviting His presence to bring transformation. It's the best medicine I know for believing lies about yourself.

If you've been told, "You're hopeless. You can't make it. You don't have it!" by a parent, brother, sister, friend, or stranger, take a long look at those words, and recognize who is behind them. Say to the devil, "Satan, I will no longer listen to lies about myself. I am not a cosmic accident, as you would have me to believe. I have worth. I have purpose. I have gifts and talents. God says that about me, and I will not contradict my heavenly Father. I rebuke your lies, and I refuse to hear them."

The Bible says, "A house divided against itself will fall" (Luke 11:17 NIV). This means that a person who has turned against himself won't make it. Much of your emotional pain may be caused by believing untrue things about yourself. Many times God was the *only* one who believed in me, but that was enough. I know now that because I believe in Him and He believes in me, I *can* make it. So can *you!*

Total wholeness and restoration was God's plan for your life from the beginning, and you should live in confidence about that. He has said many wonderful things in His Word about you, and I have listed seven very important ones in this chapter. Read through them and check to make sure you are living as though you believe each one of them. This is the truth about *you!*

Over the years I have walked with God, He has always kept His promises to me, and He has always come through. Many times it didn't feel as if He was going to, but He did. It didn't always happen the way I was wanting it to, or as quickly as I wanted to see things happen. And, thank God, it wasn't to the degree I envisioned. It was always far *better.* His timing was perfect and His way was right! Everything I have received from the Lord and more, I want for you.

If at any time you become overwhelmed by how much you think you have to do to arrive at emotional wholeness, or if you have doubts about whether you can do all that's necessary, then you need to remind yourself that *it is the Holy Spirit who accomplishes wholeness in you.* Let *Him* do it. Tell God that you want *His* ways to become *your* ways so that you can move into all the wholeness He has for you.

Prayer

Lord, help me to stand strong in You. Give me endurance to run the race and not give up. Strengthen me for the battle and help me to rise again if I fall. I look to You as my Healer and Restorer. Make me the whole person You created me to be.

Seven Things God Says Are True About Me

1. *I am a child of God, and my inheritance comes from Him.*
   "But as many as received Him, to them He gave the right to become children of God, even to those who believe in His name" (John 1:12).

2. *I have a special, God-ordained purpose.*
   "Eye has not seen, nor ear heard, nor have entered into the heart of man the things which God has prepared for those who love Him" (1 Cor. 2:9).

3. *I have been created with a specific calling.*
   "Each one has his own gift from God" (1 Cor. 7:7).

4. *I am never alone.*
   "I am with you always, even to the end of the age" (Matt. 28:20).

5. *I am never forgotten.*
   "God has not cast away His people whom He foreknew" (Rom. 11:2).

6. *I am loved.*
   "As the Father loved Me, I also have loved you" (John 15:9).

7. *I am a winner.*
   "In all these things we are more than conquerors through Him who loved us" (Rom. 8:37).

What the Bible Says About Becoming All God Made You to Be

If anyone is in Christ, he is a new creation; old things have passed away; behold, all things have become new.

—2 Corinthians 5:17

Do not remember the former things, nor consider the things of old. Behold, I will do a new thing, now it shall spring forth; shall you not know it? I will even make a road in the wilderness and rivers in the desert.

—Isaiah 43:18–19

Most assuredly, I say to you, he who hears My word and believes in Him who sent Me has everlasting life, and shall not come into judgment, but has passed from death into life.

—John 5:24

The LORD shall preserve your going out and your coming in from this time forth, and even forevermore.

—Psalm 121:8

You are complete in Him.

—Colossians 2:10

Arise, shine; For your light has come! And the glory of the LORD is risen upon you.

—Isaiah 60:1

About The Author

Stormie Omartian is a popular writer, accomplished song-writer, speaker, and author of ten books. Her other books include *Just Enough Light for the Step I'm On*, the bestselling 1998 Gold Medallion finalist *The Power of a Praying Wife*, *The Power of a Praying Parent*, *That's What Love Is For*, *Greater Health God's Way*, *Child of the Promise*, and *Stormie*, the story of her journey from the brokenness of being an abused child to becoming a whole person.

A popular media guest, Stormie has appeared on numerous radio and television programs, including *The 700 Club*, *Parent Talk*, *Homelife*, *Crosstalk*, and *Today's Issues*. Stormie speaks all over the United States in churches, women's retreats, and conferences. For twenty years Stormie has been encouraging women to pray for their families. She desires to help others become all that God created them to be, to establish strong family bonds and marriages, and to be instruments of God's love.

Stormie has been married to Grammy-winning record producer Michael Omartian for nearly thirty years. They have three grown children, Christopher, Amanda, and John David.

You can contact Stormie through her Web site:

STORMIEOMARTIAN@aol.com.